Slavery in Texas

Johanna Rosa Engelking

Slavery in Texas
Johanna Rosa Engelking

Based on a thesis Submitted to the department of history of Baylor University in partial fulfilment of the requirements for the degree of Master of Arts
AUGUST, 1933
With a short biography and edited by
Stephen A. Engelking MBA

© 2022 Texianer Verlag
Tuningen
Germany
www.texianer.com

ISBN: 978-3-949-197-9-63

Cover Illustration: *The Old Plantation* attributed to John Rose—Creative Commons PD-ART

To
CONRAD PHILLIP ENGELKING
My brother, whose encouragement and cooperation
have assisted me in doing this work.

Acknowledgment is due to Dr. Francis Gevrier
Guittard, Chairman of the Department of History of
Baylor University, for his patient and courteous direction
in the writing of this thesis, and to Mrs. Hatcher,
Librarian of State Archives, for her untiring helpfulness.

Contents

A Short Biography...7

Introduction..13

Chapter I Slavery in Texas under Spain........................17
> Extent of Slavery; Slave Trade;
> Royal Order of 1818; Number of Slaves in Texas

Chapter II Slavery in Texas from 1821-1836.................21
> American Settlements in Texas; Colonization Laws in Regard to Slavery; Review of Slavery Question by Colonists; Revision of Slavery Laws; Evasion of Slave Laws by Texas Colonists; Austin's Colony; Bill of Sale of Slaves

Chapter III The Republic and Slavery............................35
> Causes of Texas Revolution; Laws In Regard to Smuggling Slaves; Edward's Scheme of Importation of Slaves into Texas; Slave Population; Treatment of Slaves; Sale of Slaves; Petitions to Congress Asking for Special Privileges for Certain Slaves

Chapter IV Annexation and the Slavery Question.........47
> Attempts of United States to Acquire Texas; Opinion of American Statesmen on the Question of Slavery and Annexation; Border Raids between Louisiana and Texas; Texas Rejection of Annexation; British Plan of Abolition of Slaves in America; The South In Favor of Annexation of Texas; President Jones' Valedictory Address

Chapter V Texas Plantations...57
> Distribution of Plantations; Location and Description of Old Plantations; Life on the Plantation; Plantation Rules; Daily Occupation Record; Record of Cotton Picking; Daily Routine of Slaves

Chapter VI Slavery During Texas Statehood.................71

>Tax Collector's Receipt; Texas Slave Population; Principal Slave-Holding Counties; Sale of Slaves; Laws Regulating Slave Hiring; Manumission

Chapter VII The Emancipation of Slaves in Texas........81

>Anti-Slavery Societies; The Work of Abolitionists; Texas' Withdrawal from the Union; Declaration of Causes of Secession; President Lincoln's Call for Volunteers; Texas' Part in the Civil War; Life on the Plantations During the Civil War; Traffic in Slaves Continues during the War; Downfall of the Southern Confederacy; General Gordon's Entry into Texas; Celebration of "Juneteenth"; Reconstruction Ordeals; The Negro and His Place in the South

Appendix...97

Bibliography...161

A Short Biography[1]

Johanna Rosa (Hannah) Engelking (1879-1966) was born in Millheim Texas in 1879 to Sigismund Engelking (1843-1905) and Anna Zimmerman (1851-1908).

Anna Zimmerman Engelking

Her father encouraged her to take the state teacher's examination – not surprising from a family much concerned with education[2]. In fact he tutored her to the point where she could take the state teacher's examination[3]. Johanna's pioneer grandfather had in fact founded the first grammar school (gymnasium) in Texas in Millheim conducted by Ernst Gustav Maetze, a highly educated political refugee from Germany. Her brother Sigismund Jr. apparently was so passionate about Shakespeare that he would deliver the Bard's words standing on his dining-table chair.[4] So she grew up in an atmosphere of education and intellectual pursuits.

However, it seems that love threatened to get in the way of her career when she was engaged to a pharmacist. She was devastated when she found out that he had been unfaithful to her and she never became involved in a relationship after that – staying single for the rest of her life (apparently so did he).

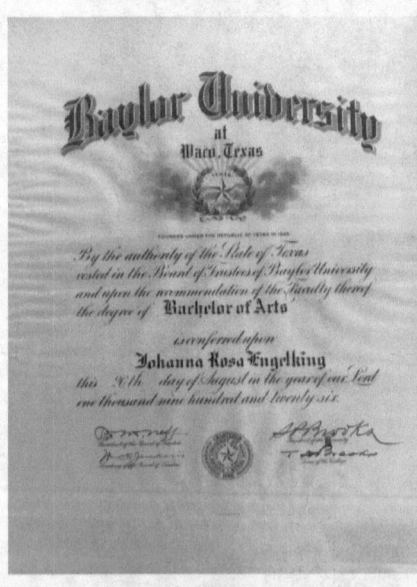

Bachelor Degree

Subsequently she studied Summer Normals to gain her B.A and then an M.A. at Baylor University (her Master's thesis is the source of this book).

Upon qualifying she embarked on what was to become a very successful teaching career over a period of fifty years. One report tells that she initially taught near Brenham Texas at Watson Lake yet I have not been able to locate that but her niece reports that she taught at Alexander Hamilton Junior High Houston and in Richards Texas. She was a highly active and assertive woman and involved herself in the Baptist Church and alumni and the Baylor Historical Society. From 1924 onwards she lived in the Rice

Hotel in Houston and it seems that she occupied a staff accommodation rather than a luxury suite where she was permitted to have a two ring cooking stove and some of her own few possessions.

Being a skilled seamstress, she made most of her niece Martha's clothes. She would go to the department store and they allowed her to make drawings so that she could reproduce them herself. Martha relates that she was very close to her and her mother and was more like a grandmother figure in her life. Apparently she could be quite pedantic and assertive, demanding a certain correctness as well as insisting on appropriate service and quality.

Apparently, she was also a good cook. Of course she did not have the facilities where she lived but was known for preparing great dishes when she visited her relatives in the summer. Her uncle Hermann had a peach orchard and she was famous for her peach strudel which she would prepare when there.

Johanna's Rocking Chair from the Rice Hotel

The Engelking family has a treasured cemetery in Millheim and she was a key figure in ensuring its preservation. This cemetery was awarded a historical marker in 2003 and is maintained to this day by the family. Apart from it holding the graves of her own ancestors it is also remarkable and unique for also having the grave of an old slave name "Uncle

Wash", who had saved her father's life and probably the rest of the family when attacked by Indians. It may be that this historical event influenced her to choose the subject of slavery for her thesis.

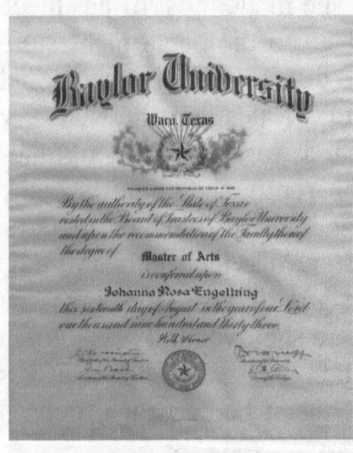

Master's Degree

Upon her retirement in 1950, she travelled around visiting relatives and collecting data for a family history. Later she was involved in the Cat Spring Agricultural Society and was decisive in the production of their important historical publications. In the Acknowledgements to *The Cat Spring Story* we read: "Members of the Cat Spring Agricultural Society are indebted to Johanna Rosa Engelking for months of effort in gathering facts on the families of the early settlers of Cat Spring and their descendants".

She kept up friendships with professors at Baylor, in particular Dr. Frank Guittard.

One of her famous colleagues during over 27 years teaching in Houston was Lyndon B. Johnson who was teaching at the Sam Houston High School and who she had introduced to her second cousin and son of the famous Robert Justus Kleberg, Richard Miffin Kleberg. This was in 1930 after he had graduated from Southwest Texas State University in San Marcos, He briefly taught public speaking at Sam Houston High. After Kleberg was elected to the U.S. Congress, he hired Johnson as his secretary, who then moved to Washington DC in 1931. Johnson wrote to Johanna later, after he had been elected

President, telling her that she was one of those responsible for his success in politics. After Johanna Rosa Engelking died at the age of 88, Johnson sent flowers to the funeral. Martha Rutherford relates that LBJ invited J. Rosa to the White House and was going to send a Presidential plane to fly her there. Unfortunately, she passed away before that trip could happen.

It is a strange matter of fact that whilst Johanna was living in the Rice Hotel[5], President J.F. Kennedy attended a conference of the League of United Latin American Citizens (LULAC) there on November 21, 1963 – the day before he was assassinated in Dallas! Kennedy used a suite at the Rice Hotel to hold meetings, which was supplied with caviar and he had been there on a number of previous occasions, where he would be served champagne, and his favorite beer. Whether he knew Johanna via President Johnson and was able to take time out to visit her on that or one of the previous occasions is a matter of speculation.[6]

Johanna Engelking in later years with her great niece Martha Susan Rutherford Butler

Money had never played an important role in her generous life and her assets did not even suffice to pay for her funeral. She never owned any property or a car and was known for her generosity. She helped many young persons through their education and when she dies, she left only her few items in her hotel room to her niece.

We hope this book will play some tribute to a life lived well for Texas education and culture.

Stephen A. Engelking

Introduction

As far back as the beginnings of history, slaves are found in all countries. In Egypt slaves toiled to build the pyramids; in Babylon the slaves are met; in Assyria on the clay tablets may be seen that a man and a camel alike sold for a half a shekel of silver; and early in Jewish history Joseph was taken from the pit and sold by his brothers.

For more than a thousand years slavery held sway in Greece and Rome. Athens was founded upon it, although she gloried in the principle of freedom; and even Aristotle, her greatest philosopher, accepted slavery as a necessity. In Rome the victorious conquerors brought home thousands of captives to serve in the houses and on the estates of the wealthy, one man sometimes owning thousands of slaves.

After the barbarian invasion of the fifth and sixth century A.D., chattel slavery gradually died out. In its place arose a new institution—the serfdom of the Middle Ages. The serf was not the chattel or "thing" of his master; he was a person, although of inferior rank.

The person of the serf was unfree, and he was "bound to the soil," and could not leave his master's estate. In England serfdom died out soon after the great Peasant Revolt in 1381, but in certain parts of France it lasted until the French Revolution. In Prussian Germany serfs were not freed until the beginning of the nineteenth century; and in Russia the great step which emancipated 40,000,000 serfs by imperial edict was not taken until 1861.

Slavery revived somewhat in Europe, especially in the

fifteenth century, when the Portuguese began to introduce African slaves taken by the expeditions which they were slowly pushing down the west African coast.

In the New World, the institution was revived with all its ancient horrors, to work the mines and till some tropical lands. At first the Spaniards tried to enslave the Indians, but they were not suited to such labor. Negro slaves were then imported from Africa. The blacks proved equal to the tasks; they were accustomed to the hot sun and became docile under cruel treatment.

An epoch making event in United States History was in 1619 when the first negro slaves were introduced into Virginia. Guilty of nothing but "a skin not colored like our own," millions of Africans were torn from their homes, and European ship-owners vied with one another for the opportunity of trading in these "cargoes of despair."

Finally the indignation of all thinking people was aroused and in 1792, Denmark took the lead in abolishing the slave-trade. Other European nations followed, and in 1815 the traffic received its final blow in the Council of Vienna when all the powers represented agreed to abolish it.

The evils of slavery, however, could be ended only with abolition. Great Britain won the distinction of being the first great modern nation to take such a step. Its example was gradually followed by the other European countries. The United States for some years remained the only important nation which still clung to slavery.

In the British colonies of North America conditions in the colonies in the North were such as to render slavery unprofitable. This is the chief reason for the exclusion of slavery from these colonies, and for more than fifty years after the Revolutionary War there was no general opposition to slavery in the North.

The development of slavery in the colonies in the South

and later in the Southern States was due solely to economic conditions. Texas was settled mostly by people from the Southern States who brought their slaves with them as they immigrated. Slavery was deemed necessary from the economic viewpoint of the first settlers in Texas, as the province was entirely agricultural and the services of slaves seemed indispensable.

The slavery question in Texas was the dominating one throughout its whole history from the time that it was settled as a Mexican colony through the Reconstruction Period after the Civil War.

Chapter I
Slavery in Texas under Spain

Extent of Slavery; Slave Trade;
Royal Order of 1818; Number of Slaves in Texas

Spain held as one of her possessions in the New World the territory known as Mexico of which Texas was one of its provinces. How Mexico gained her independence from Spain and how later, in turn, Texas became independent of Mexico is irrelevant, as this theme deals only with the institution of slavery as related to Texas.

Slavery in Texas during the Spanish rule was far from being extensive. There were a few slaves who were the descendants of conquered Indians, but usually when we refer to slaves, we mean the negroes of African descent or native Africans sold into slavery.

Slavery as an institution hardly existed in the province of Texas at this time, but a far greater evil did exist, and it was that of the slave trade carried on with the United States by means of capturing the poor victims in Africa and then transporting them to Galveston Island and smuggling them into Louisiana.

Lafitte was stationed on Galveston Island and it was through the operation of his three most successful salesmen, the three Bowie brothers—Resin P., James, and John J.—that large profits were made from the slave trade.

The importation of slaves was prohibited in the United States, but the Bowie brothers devised a scheme by means of which this slave-trade could be carried on in such a manner as seemingly not to directly violate the laws of either country; shrewdness was one of the characteristics of Lafitte and his men.

Custom officers were stationed along the Louisiana border, and one of their duties was to intercept imported slaves. After the interception of these unfortunate human beings, the officers took charge of them as smuggled property and sold them later at auction to the highest bidder.[7]

The Bowie brothers would sell slaves to Louisiana Companies, who, wishing to validate their titles to them that they might safely ship them up the Mississippi River, surrendered them to the Custom officers, who, according to law, resold them as "smuggled slaves." The Louisiana Companies always bought them back, and received as informers, a rebate of half their purchase money.

Slaves, at this time, were always sold by the pound; the established price was a dollar per pound for young healthy Africans. The Bowie brothers would keep the Africans for a while in order to have them put on as much weight as possible and thereby be of greater value when sold. The average slave weighed about 158 pounds when sold. The profits on slaves from the years 1818 to 1820 amounted to over $6500[8].

By royal order, in 1818, the Spanish monarch had strictly forbidden the importation of slaves or their sale in Mexico or any other colony. The Cominician provincial of Chiapas, Father Katias Cordoba, gave freedom to the slaves on the estates of his order, and President Victoria had liberated in the country's name the slaves purchased with certain funds collected for that purpose, as well as those given up by their owners to the patriotic junta.[9]

The few slaves that were in Texas at this time were centered at De Bexar and at Nacogdoches. For practical purposes there were no slaves in Texas until immigrants from the United States brought them. Fifteen slaves, who had run away from their masters in Louisiana, were listed in 1808 as being at Nacogdoches and the Trinity River bottom.[10] Residents around San Antonio held a few slaves; the census report in 1819 shows five male slaves and two female slaves there; these slaves were personal servants and were not employed for economic reasons.[11]

However, when the Spanish authorities issued the grant to settle colonists in Texas to Moses Austin, they thereby recognized slavery. Again they recognized the institution of slavery when Stephen F. Austin secured ratification to the grant which his father had previously obtained from Spain and in this said grand was the provision that each settler was to be allowed eighty acres of land for each slave that accompanied him.[12]

Chapter II
Slavery in Texas from 1821-1836

American Settlements in Texas; Colonization Laws in Regard to Slavery; Review of Slavery Question by Colonists; Revision of Slavery Laws; Evasion of Slave Laws by Texas Colonists; Austin's Colony; Bill of Sale of Slaves

In the year 1821 Mexico gained her independence from Spain, and it was also the year in which Moses Austin's petition for permission to settle an Anglo-American colony in Texas was officially granted by the Mexican government; no mention of slavery was made in either petition or grant.

Upon the death of Moses Austin, his son, Stephen F. Austin, was given permission to carry out the grant given to his father. The governor of Texas acting as agent for Mexico gave his approval for the distribution of land as drawn up by the plan of Stephen F. Austin. This plan consisted, as far as slavery was concerned, of a grant of land of eighty acres for each slave belonging to the family emigrating to Austin's colony. Most of Austin's colonists were families from the southern portion of the United States and most of them owned a small number of slaves. Later, the governor of Texas refused to give these grants of land, and not an acre of land ever was distributed according to Austin's plan as regards to slave ownership.

Stephen F. Austin went to the Mexican capital in March, 1822, where he found Mexico all in confusion and Congress busy framing colonization laws. The question of slavery presented the greatest obstacle to the passage of the laws. The colonization laws were very important to Austin and the slave question had to be settled. Austin was a firm believer in the necessity of slaves, while Mexico, having just gained her freedom from Spain, wanted to pass on the boon. Mexico believed in liberation, and as there existed only a few slaves in her territory, the question was an abstract one with Mexico.

Three colonization laws were offered in Congress: (1) A bill that was silent as to the subject of slavery except as to cities, declaring that foreigners might be allowed the privilege of founding cities only on condition of adopting the Spanish language and freeing their slaves. (2) A bill for immediate emancipation. (3) A bill reported by the Committee on Colonization that contained a clause to the effect that slaves introduced into the Empire by colonists should remain so for life, and their children born in the Empire should gain their independence at the age of fourteen years. During the debate that followed the introduction of these bills, no one was willing to make any greater concessions. Congress reached the Colonization Law in August, 1822, but not much mention of slavery was made. The bill proved unsatisfactory and was recommitted with certain instructions, none of which concerned slavery.

Iturbide, who was emperor, provoked a crisis on October 30, 1822, when he drove the members of Congress out of doors at the point of the bayonet. The emperor then organized a Junta of thirty-five members which took up legislative matters. The article on slavery reached discussion on November 26, 1822. All seemed anxious to secure total abolition, but were inclined to pay due regard to the right which masters had acquired under existing laws. Señor Parras alone presented the subject from the point of view of the colonists. He explained that due to the great scarcity of labor in the new settlements, the colonists would be unwilling to remove to the Mexican provinces unless protection in ownership of their slaves was made, and that there would be sufficient safeguards by prohibiting slave-trade and the emancipation of children of slaves at the age of fourteen.

The article finally passed was: "There shall not be permitted, after the promulgation of this law, either purchase or sale of slaves that may be introduced into the empire. The children of such slaves, who are born within the empire, shall be free at fourteen years of age."[13]

Passage of the above bill was due to the tact and energy of Stephen F. Austin. An excerpt of a letter from Austin of January 8, 1823, to Governor Trespalacious, reads: "I talked to every member of the Junta upon the necessity which exists in Texas, Santander, and all the other uninhabited provinces, that the new colonists should be permitted to bring their slaves, and in this manner, I procured the article.[14] It seems that Austin's persistent lobbying carried the measure through the Junta.

The complete colonization law was promulgated by the Emperor on January 4, 1823. It was annulled after the overthrow of Iturbide, and by special decree of the government Stephen F. Austin's grant was confirmed and he was allowed to go forward with the settlement under the provisions of the annulled law. Thus the government of Mexico, while all buoyant with the hopes born of revolution and moved by theories of equality of brotherhood of man, authorized the introduction of negro slavery into one of its fairest provinces.

The Congress of Coahuila and Texas expressly gave the colonists permission to bring in their slaves for six months after the publication of the State Constitution of 1827. The thirteenth article, as it was finally adopted and as it appeared in the Constitution which was published on March

11, 1827, reads as follows:

> "Article XIII: From and After the promulgation of the Constitution in the capital of each district, no one shall be born a slave in the state, and after six months, the introduction of slaves under any pretext shall not be permitted."[15]

After six months, Congress issued a decree for carrying into effect the provisions of the above article. Municipalities were ordered to make a list of all slaves within their limits; deaths and births were to be reported to the state government every three months and a careful register of the same was to be kept by the ayuntamientos.

Some other laws and provisions were that a tenth of the slaves must be emancipated whenever ownership changed, which, of course, would be only by inheritance, the ayuntamientos were also required to provide for "the best education that can be given" to the emancipated children. The slave was allowed to change his master, provided the new master would indemnify the old master.

In the Laws and Decrees of Coahuila and Texas are found the following articles:[16]

> "Article IV: Those who introduce slaves, after the expiration of the term specified in Article XIII of the Constitution, shall be subject to the penalties established by the general law of the thirteenth of July, 1824.
>
> "Article V: Slaves, whose owners have no heirs apparent according to the existing laws, shall be immediately free on the death of their masters, and shall not pass to any other kind of succession whatever under any aspect.
>
> "Article VI: The Manumission mentioned in the preceding article shall not take place when the master, or

his heirs, are poisoned or assassinated by one of their slaves; in that case they shall be subject to the provision of the laws.

"Article VII: In each change of owner of slaves, in the nearest succession, even of heirs apparent, the tenth part of those to pass to the new owner, shall be manumitted; the said portion to be determined by lot before the Ayuntamiento of the municipal district.

"Article VIII: Children and parents by adoption shall not mutually inherit slave property.

"Article IX: The Ayuntamientos, under their most rigid responsibility, shall take particular care that free children, born of slaves, receive the best education that can be given them; placing them, for that purpose, at the public schools and other places of instruction, wherein they may become useful to society.

"Article X: Ayuntamientos that shall not be faithful in the fulfillment of this law, shall suffer a fine of $500, which the Executive shall order appropriated to the benefit of Public Schools.

"Article XI: This law shall be first published in this town on the morrow, and in the other towns on the day following the receipt thereof. The same shall be republished annually on the sixteenth of September until the year 1840.

"For its fulfillment, the governor of the state shall cause it to be printed, published, and circulated.

> "Given in Satillo on the 15th of Sept., 1827
> Ramon Garcia Rojas, President
> Juan A. Gonzales, D. S.
> Miguel Arcineaga, D. S."

The native inhabitants of Mexico were almost to a man opposed to slavery. The system had been totally abolished in every section of the Republic but Texas. The

Constitution of the Mexican Republic adopted in 1824 expressly provided that no person should thereafter be born a slave or introduced as such in the Mexican states; that all slaves then held should receive stipulated wages and be subject to no punishment but upon trial and judgment of magistrates.

As early as 1826, slave owners talked of leaving Texas rather than have their slaves emancipated. Slaves had been guaranteed to the settlers by the Law of Colonization, and they argued that they could and should not be deprived of them. It would be an unjust abuse of the rights of the colonists; slaves were considered indispensable to the prosperity of colonists in Texas.[17]

Stephen Fuller Austin, the founder of the Anglo-American colonization of Texas, was himself a slave owner. His father, Moses Austin, had also used slave labor in his lead mines in Virginia and in Missouri.

People who wished to emigrate from the United States to Texas always reviewed the slavery question and the laws of Mexico.[18] To Stephen F. Austin and other men who looked toward the future from an economic viewpoint, it seemed evident that if the Mexican government wished to have that fine territory of the colonies changed from a savage wilderness to a populous, civilized, and cultivated state capable of contributing a material quota towards national income, wealth, and prosperity, slaves must be tolerated in these colonies.

Settlers from the Southern States were best, suited to develop this territory through slave labor on cotton plantations and Austin expressed his opinion that property in slaves should be guaranteed.[19]

A decree of May 5, 1828, which again opened Texas to slavery, reads:

"The Congress of the State of Coahuila and Texas, attending to the deficiency of workingmen to give activity to agriculture and the other arts, and desiring to facilitate their introduction into the state, as well as the growth and prosperity of said branches, has thought proper to decree: All contracts, not in opposition to the laws of the state, that have been entered into in foreign countries between emigrants who came to settle in this state, or between the inhabitants thereof, and the servants and day laborers or workingmen whom they introduce, are hereby guaranteed to be valid in said state."[20]

Negro laborers were needed for large plantations. Austin thought that the decree was a permit for necessary house servants and laborers. Austin's colony was purely an agricultural one, and unless the plantations could be tilled, there was no subsistence for the colonists, much less a future. Economic, as well as social Conditions, demanded servants and laborers.

On September 15, 1829, the anniversary of Mexican Independence, President Guerrero in conformity to an article in the Federal Constitution empowering him to that effect, issued a decree totally and immediately abolishing slavery throughout the Republic.

A change in the administration of the government took place soon after, and representations were made to the general Congress, setting forth that many of the slaves introduced by the Texas colonists were so extremely ignorant as to unfit them for their freedom, and a dispensation of the aforesaid decree was granted so far only as related to Texas. The former system was revived in that particular section of the country and the slaves introduced previous to the year 1824 were legally held as apprentices.

The colonists then adopted the plan of taking in slaves

under formal indentures, for long periods, in order to evade the law.

The State Legislature passed a law as soon as the facts were made known to it, requiring the registration of all slaves that had been legally imported, and declaring that no indenture should, in any case whatsoever, be obligatory upon others than a period of ten years. It was also provided by law that all children of persons thus in the condition of apprentices, should be free from the control of those held to be their parents at the age of fourteen years and be placed by the municipal authorities under the control of suitable persons, to learn some useful trade or industrious occupation and receive a portion of common school education.

Early in 1830 the Legislature of Louisiana ordered expulsion of all free negroes and mulattoes who had illegally entered the state, but instead of offering inducements to these free negroes, the Mexican vice-consul at New Orleans published notices that such negroes were strictly forbidden to enter Texas, and that shipmasters could not land them on the coast of Texas.

At this time there were but very few free negroes in Texas, and perhaps it would have been far wiser for the Mexican government to have induced these free negroes to come to Texas and thereby have given the colonists in Texas an opportunity to employ negro help, other than slaves, to cultivate the fertile lands of the river bottoms that did not seem adapted to the habitation and cultivation by the colonists themselves.

Lawful slavery was confined to the African race and a child could only be a slave if born by a slave mother. Where Chickasaw Indians had given negroes their freedom prior to 1821-1822, the state had no right to interfere. No proof could be established that the Indians forbade manumission of slaves.[21]

There is no doubt that the Texans evaded the law prohibiting the further introduction of slavery, but it must be added that they did so with the express consent and connivance of the state government. It was a unique plan by which negroes were brought into Texas after the decree of May, 1828. Prior to leaving the United States, the master and the slave appeared before a Notary Public, or some other official whose seal would give validity to the document, and in the most formal manner gave their adhesion to the agreement, which was duly signed and witnessed.

The document usually begins with the statement that the negro is held as a slave under the existing laws of the state in which the contract is drawn up; that he desires to accompany his master to Texas, where he will receive his freedom on entering the state; and that by the way of compensating his master, he agrees to pay in labor the sum at which he is valued, plus the cost of removal to Texas. The necessary cost of clothing, food, and other necessities is to be deducted from his wages as first charge. The wages named in a blank form found among Austin's papers is $20 per year.

> "And furthermore (states the contract) the said slave being desirous that his child, or children, should enjoy the benefits of the said states of Coahuila and Texas, and that he, or they, should be removed by the same said master therefore, as parent and natural guardian, he, the said slave, contracts and agrees with the said master that his child or children shall serve on the same terms as the father, wages to begin when the child reaches the age of eighteen years." The contract even anticipates the birth of other children after the removal to Texas, and provides that "they shall serve the master till they are twenty-five years old without wages, this being in consideration of the benefits they receive from

the removal of their parent by said master, and which they never could have enjoyed unless it had been secured to them by this contract, under which said master was induced to remove the said slave to said state of Coahuila and Texas.

"After the expiration of twenty-five years, the children born after removal are to continue serving on the same terms as the father, until all debts due the master are paid. The master is held bound to instruct said children in some useful branch of industry that will make them useful members of the community. And said slave generally contracts and agrees with the said master faithfully to serve him or his representatives as a servant and laborer as above stated, and to be obedient and submissive as a good and faithful servant should be, and faithfully to comply with this contract under the penalty of ___dollars."[22]

These contracts properly signed and witnessed made the negro thus brought into Texas as truly a slave as if his master had remained in the United States. The negro could never pay the debt acknowledged in the agreement, or even that contracted from year to year in clothing and other necessities. Under this legalized evasion of the law, the Texas immigrants continued to bring in their slaves, and the agitation of the subject subsided for a year or two.[23]

Besides the slaves that were brought in from the United States, there was that class of slaves that were occasionally smuggled in from the West Indies and who were newly acquired Africans as a rule. Negroes, who were bought from importers and carried home by the purchasers, were ordinarily treated differently from the old ones. They were only gradually accustomed to work. They were made to bathe often; to take walks from time to time, and especially to dance. They were distributed in small numbers among old slaves in order to dispose them better to acquire their habits. Often, poor masters who had no other slaves, or who were too greedy, would require hard labor of these newly acquired negroes, and thereby exhaust them quickly, lose them by sickness and more often by grief.[24]

The convention of 1833 offered and passed strong resolutions prohibiting slave traffic. Unprincipled men had been in this business for the sake of gain, although some of them had been arrested and hanged by the British cruisers.

Austin, who at first was sincere in his doubts as regards negro slavery, seems to have been entirely convinced by 1833 that Texas should be a slave country. In 1825 the population of Austin's Colony numbered 1800 white persons and 443 slaves against 8000 white persons and 1000 slaves in the year 1834.[25]

In 1834 three Political Divisions were established in Texas: Bexar, Brazos, and Nacogdoches. In the Bexar Department there were mostly Mexicans and Almonte claimed there were no negro laborers; however, there were a few household servants of African race. The Department of Nacogdoches had four municipalities, namely: Nacogdoches, San Augustine, Liberty, and Jonesboro; the population was 9,000, including 1,000 negroes. The exports were estimated at 2,000 bales of cotton, 90,000 skins of deer, otter, and beaver, besides 5,000 cattle.[26] The towns were Anahuac, Bevil, Teran, and Teneha.

The Department of Brazos had a population of about 8,000, of which 1,000 were slaves. It was in this Department that Austin's Colony was located. The municipalities were San Felipe, Columbia, Matagorda, Gonzales, and Mina, with the towns of Brazoria, Harrisburg, Velasco, and Bolivar. Almonte reported exports of about 2,000 bales of cotton in 1833 from the Department of Brazos to New Orleans at from ten to ten and a half cents per pound after paying two and one-half cents per pound duty in New Orleans.[27]

At this time the Texas farms were cultivated by the farmer with his slaves, the farmer working by the side of his slaves; there were no extensive slave-holders in Texas then, usually only one negro family.[28] People lived on what the slaves produced for each farmer. The land was cheap and fertile and the slaves attended, with the help of their owners, to the cultivation of the crops of cotton, corn, cane, and large plots of sweet potatoes; corn and sweet potatoes were the staple food of the plantation. Besides the cultivation of crops, the slaves split rails; tore down and built fences; made and cleaned out ditches; shelled corn; killed hogs; hauled wood; kept birds from corn coming up; worked roads; built chimneys; killed beeves; attended to raising hogs, and any other work on the farm necessary to be done. But there was no work done on Sunday.[29]

The following are exact copies of some of the letters exchanged between colonists in Texas and their relatives and friends in the United States:

Excerpt from a letter from Stephen F. Austin to James E. Brown when they were making plans to move Austin's widow and his widowed sister, Mrs. Emily Margaret Bryan, from Missouri to Texas:

> "I am in favor of your coming by land; bring the family of negroes that Emily has at all hazards and I will settle with Bryan for them. If you can get Luck and Babtiste and Pool without paying too much, money, do so."[30]

William Brenaugh to Austin:
"Natchitoches March 19, 1825"

"Sir: It is my wish to procure land in your country. I am a man of family, have twelve negroes and will improve the same within the time prescribed by law. I authorize Mr. Smith to locate it for me.
Wm. Brenaugh
Mr. S. F. Austin"[31]
"Austin to Jared E. Grace:
I have this day hired three negroes from Jared E. Grace—to wit a negro woman called Sally, a negro man called tame Jack and one called Kelley—the woman at eight dollars per month and the men at fifteen each—the hire to commence on the first day of November next, and continue for one year from that date, and I hereby obligate myself to pay to said Grace the amount of said hire at the expiration of the year— A Boy called Fields is to be furnished to take care of Sally's child—The said negroes are to be well treated by me, and the said Grace is to clothe them—Should they run away or die the loss is to be Grace's—sickness to be my loss.
Brazos River — October 19, 1823
Stephen F. Austin
October 19th 1823 the negroes is to be returned when the hire ceases.
S. F. Austin Rubric[32]

In another excerpt from a letter of Austin where the question of a settlement of a debt is involved, we find "that no credit will be given for lands and nothing taken in payment but money or negroes."[33]

"Contract for Hire of Slaves
Know all men by these presents that whereas Robert H. Williams has received by me the sum of three hundred and Twenty Dollars in three equal annual pay-

ments I hereby transfer and set over to him by Right and Claim to the services of a certain negro man named Harry for the time of three Years from the date of these presents given under my hand and seal this 3rd day of December 1824
Felix H. Walker Seal
"For value received I transfer the within to Stephen F. Austin—San Felipe de Austin Ho. 15, 1825"[34]

Excerpt from a letter of Austin to Perry, March 3, 1832:

"McKinstre has a very likely negro, 27 years of age, healthy and a good field hand, he has ran away owing to a terrible whipping Mc gave him the other day, but I believe he has no very bad habits—he asks $1200 cash."[35]

Slaves were bought and sold freely and negroes were even given in payment for horses and mules.[36]

Slavery continued to exist in Texas in spite of all the laws forbidding such that were passed by the Mexican government, and the unwillingness of the colonists of Texas to part with their slaves, was one of the foremost causes of the Revolutionary War with Mexico.

Chapter III
The Republic and Slavery

Causes of Texas Revolution; Laws In Regard to Smuggling Slaves; Edward's Scheme of Importation of Slaves into Texas; Slave Population; Treatment of Slaves; Sale of Slaves; Petitions to Congress Asking for Special Privileges for Certain Slaves

Texas, the Lone Star Republic, gained its independence from Mexico in the year of 1836.

Presumedly the war for independence was waged by the colonists and their leaders as a revolt against the oppression of Mexico, but in reality, one of the underlying causes was the agitation in the United States of those who saw in Texas a splendid opportunity for slave trade.

> "A review of facts and circumstances showing that this contest is a crusade against Mexico, set on foot and supported by slaveholders in order to reestablish, extend, and perpetuate the system of slavery and of slave-trade."[37]

Many of the substantial colonists were opposed to the War with Mexico, but among the settlers of the colonies were ambitious aspirants from the United States of the North. Mexico would not voluntarily cede Texas to the United States.

Mr. Upshur, a member of the Virginia Convention in 1829 said in that body: "Nothing is more fluctuating than the value of slaves. A late law of Louisiana reduced their value twenty-five per cent in two hours after its passage was known. If it should be our lot, as I trust it will, to acquire Texas, their price will rise."[38]

Mr. Doddridge, another member of the same convention made a similar declaration: "that the acquisition of Texas would greatly enhance the property in question."[39]

Sam Houston came to Texas to revolutionize it. President Jackson saw that the vast territory of Texas would not fail to exercise an important and favorable influence upon the future destinies of the South by increasing the votes of the slaveholding states in the United States Senate.

Colonel Butler, the Charge d'Affairs of the United States to Mexico, was especially authorized by the President to treat with that governor for the purchase of Texas; but this could not be done and the United States had to wait either until a more friendly party was in power, or Texas was independent.

The famous Senator in Congress, Thos. H. Benton, called Texas the cradle for slaves and that these could be supplied faster from Texas than from foreign countries.

When Texas gained her independence from Mexico, there were political, social, and economical considerations that combined to render her a slave-holding country. At the time of the adoption of her Constitution, most of her inhabitants were from slave-holding states of America. These inhabitants wanted their relatives and friends to settle in Texas, but these would not come without slaves. There was an abundance of land, but a scarcity of labor. It was not easy to argue planters into the relinquishment of a right which the law and usage of his birthplace had always recognized. Geographically, Texas was not adapted to a great extension of slavery. Beyond the Rio Grande labor was abundant and people led a pastoral life. The climate North and West of Texas is not well suited to the negro.

Slaves at the time of the Revolutionary War with Mexico were used solely as laborers; this is seen, from the fact that the Provisional Government of Texas did not even require slaves to enroll for military duty. An ordinance regulating the militia reads:

> Section 1: Be it resolved and declared, and it is hereby resolved and declared by the General Council of the Provisional Government of Texas, That every free white able-bodied male inhabitant over sixteen and under fifty years of age, shall be subject to Militia Duty.[40]

During the Revolution, negroes on the Brazos made an attempt at an uprising. At Brazoria nearly one hundred negroes were taken up and whipped and some were hanged.[41]

One of the first problems to confront the new Republic was that of curbing the smuggling of negroes into Texas. On December 21, 1836, Congress passed the following Act:

> Any person or persons who introduces any African negro or negroes, contrary to the true intent and meaning of the ninth section of the general provisions of the Constitution, declaring the introduction of African Negroes into the Republic to be piracy, except such as from the United States of America, and have been held as slaves therein, shall be considered guilty of piracy; and upon conviction thereof, before any court having cognizance of the same, shall suffer death, without benefit of clergy.

This same Act likewise decreed:

> If any person or persons shall introduce into the Re-

public of Texas any Africans or any slave or slaves from the United States of America, except such slave or slaves as were previously introduced and held in slavery in that Republic, in conformity with the laws of that government, shall be deemed guilty of piracy, and upon conviction thereof, before any court having cognizance of the same, should suffer death.[42]

Sam Houston's message to Congress in 1837 has this decisive passage:

"Not unconnected with the naval force of the country is the subject of the African slave trade. It cannot be disbelieved that thousands of Africans have lately been imported to the island of Cuba, with a design to transfer a large portion of them into the Republic. The unholy and cruel traffic has called down the reprobation of the human and just of all civilized nations. Our abhorrence to it is clearly expressed in our Constitution and laws.

"Nor has it rested alone upon the declaration of our policy, but has long since been a subject of representation to the government of the United States, our Ministers apprising it of every fact which would enable it to devise such means as would prevent either the landing or introduction of Africans into our country.

"The naval force of Texas not being in a situation to be diverted from our immediate defense, will be a sufficient reason why the governments of the United States and England should employ such a portion of their force in the Gulf as will at once arrest the accursed trade and redeem this Republic from the suspicion of connivance, which would be as detrimental to its character as the practice is repugnant to the feelings of its citizens. Should the traffic continue, the odium cannot rest upon us, but will remain a blot upon the escutcheon of nations who have power, and withhold their hand from the work of humanity."[43]

The wholesale price of Africans at Havana was, according to Mr. Turnbull, 1838, about $300 a head; another $100 to he added for freight and risk of capture. Money expended on slave labor in Texas amounted to $6,000,000. No wonder the world was surprised at Texas doing this.

The British Commissioner for the suppression of slave-trade, who resided in Cuba, reported that twenty-seven slave vessels arrived in Havana in 1833; 33 in 1834; 50 in 1835; and in 1836 that more than 15,000 negroes must have been landed.

One man by the name of Taylor from the Barbadoes was convicted of sending free negroes to this new market and selling them.

In 1840 Monroe Edwards devised a scheme for the importation of slaves. Edwards entered into partnership with a man named Dart from Mississippi who furnished $30,000 for the purchase of negroes in Cuba. A slaver had been captured by a British cruiser and brought into Havana where the negroes were apprenticed for a term of years. Edwards purchased a large number of these and introduced them into Texas. It was understood between him and Dart that they were to be sent through Texas to Louisiana. Edwards though began selling them out in Texas and appropriated the funds. Dart sequestered the remaining negroes, but, on trial, Edwards, gave in evidence a full receipt from Dart for the money originally advanced.

Upon a close examination of this paper, it was found that Edwards had extracted all the writing on a letter from Dart to him, except the signature, and had written the receipt above it. Edwards was forthwith prosecuted for forgery. He gave bail and fled to the United States. In 1840, he wrote President Lamar, and also General Sam Houston, representing the facts in part, but stating that he had been defrauded in the purchase of the negroes, believing them to be slaves; that by treaty stipulations, both England and Spain were bound for the restoration of the negroes to freedom; that the British government had been fully advised of all the facts with a descriptive list of the negroes; that he was on his way to London with letters from Mr. Adams, Gen. Wilson, Mr. Fox, Dr. Channing, and twenty other gentlemen of high standing here and in Europe, to press the liberation of the negroes, and was advised that the Texas government would be held responsible for them. He further stated that he had high authority for saying that, the moment the question was agitated in London, the successful negotiation of the Texan loan was at an end; and concluded by advising that the negroes be safely kept, to abide the issue to be made by the British government.

Edwards attracted much attention by his seeming sympathy for these negroes, and acquired influence with the ministry. General Hamilton had to interpose and expose Edwards as a criminal fled from Justice in Texas.[44]

The Republic sustained itself under extraordinary difficulties. There was no means to raise currency, but each field negro in Texas produced by cultivation of cotton and Indian corn, at the lowest calculation, $500 yearly without injury to his health.

The slave population in Texas in 1839 was not more than 10,000.[45] The growth of slave population was tabulated by Almonte in his statistical surveys and reads as follows:

Year	Number of slaves
1836	5,000
1840	11,323
1841	13,000
1843	25,000
1845	28,624[46]

The life of the slave was practically about the same that it was during the time of the colonists in Texas. Slaves were hired out as needed; such emergencies were met by mutual accommodation of neighbors. An excerpt from a letter in 1836 from Edmund Andrews to Perry reads: "Have you any among those Westall's slaves that you will hire me for a cook?"[47] Hired negroes were boarded but their clothing charged to their master. If slaves worked on Sunday, which they often had to do in sugar making, they received the one dollar pay themselves.

Negroes were allowed patches of their own to cultivate, and they usually raised corn, cotton, and vegetables on these.

As to the treatment of slaves by their masters, little is revealed. The following excerpt from a letter in regard to a slave named Henderson, will give the reader an insight:

> City of Houston
> January 6, 1837
> To Wm. H. Wharton Esq.
> My very dear Sir:
> It is with great pain I inform you of the death of Henderson your servant. He died yesterday afternoon and will he buried in a coffin this morning.
> A day or two after your departure he had a severe relapse. From this he became quite convalescent and entirely free of fever. I had with him from the day you left till his death a good attendant. He was removed from the quarters to my ketchen and had every attention.[48]

Slaves were sold and Bills of Sales given.

Orizimho
July 14, 1837
Dr. Ashbell Smith
Dear Sir:
I have been informed that Dr. Goodrich has left two servants belonging to him, a man and a woman, with you at Houston for sale.
I want to purchase them—will you be kind enough to inform me what the prices of the negroes are—on what terms—and if you are authorized to sell and make title.
Very respectfully,
James W. Robinson[49]
$1500
Whereas I have this day sold to John W. Malone 3 Negroes Luly age about 21 child 18 months Lin about 16 years for the sum of Fifteen hundred dollars I warrant and defend the title against every one or all Persons Given under my hand this the 4th day of Oct 1844
Marcus Gill[50]

The following is another copy of a Bill of Sale:

November 25, 1836
George B. McKinstry to Austin
Be it Known. That in consideration of the Sum of twelve hundred dollars to me in hand paid the receipt of which is hereby acknowledged, I have this day sold to Stephen F. Austin a certain Negro Man named Simon, of a dark complexion aged about twenty-seven years. I warrant the health as well the title of said Negro against the claim of any person whatever, In witness whereof I have hereunto set my hand in the Town

of Columbia this 25th November 1836.
Geo. B. McKinstry
Witness:
Barnard E. Bee[51]

A Bill of Sale for a negro Girl:

Rutersville Fayette County May 20th 1840
Received of Charles Fordtran four hundred dollars in full for a negro girl named Margaret which negro I warrant to be sound in mind and body and also warrant her to be a slave for life and warrant and defend the title to said Fordtran his heirs or assigns forever.
Wager S. Smith
Charlotte M. C. Smith
The paid girl is about ten years old.[52]

Soundness of slave guaranteed at time of sale held for damages if proof was made that the slave died from illness that prevailed at the time of sale.[53]

Negroes were sold to satisfy a mortgage on an estate and in such a case a bill of sale was not necessary to pass the title to a slave.

The enticing away of a slave was a trespass, and where the taking was without force, but was accompanied by acts tending to a breach of the peace, it was a forcible trespass.

An interesting case is cited where Wiley Martin, who had no relatives, wished to free his slave, Peter, who had accumulated $16,000, and who had given splendid services and was of good character. This aroused a debate in the Senate and Congress finally had to pass a special law, namely:

An Act:
To authorize Wiley Martin to emancipate his slave Peter.

Section 1st: Be it enacted by the Senate and the House of Representative of the Republic of Texas in Congress assembled: That from and after the passage of this Act, that Wiley Martin is hereby authorized to Manumit and set free his Negro Slave Peter.

Section 2cd: Be it further enacted That the said Peter after his emancipation may be permitted to remain in this Republic with his property untill Congress shall direct otherwise. Provided, that the said Wiley Martin shall before emancipating, enter into bond with one good Security payable to the Chief Justice of the County of Fort Bend and his successors in office in the sum of one thousand dollars conditioned that the said Peter shall never become a charge of the said County or the Republic.

David S. Kaufman
Speaker of the House of Representative
David G. Burnet
President of the Senate
Approved 3rd January, 1840
Mirabeau B. Lamar
I certify that this act originated in the Senate
Algernon Thompson
Ass. Sec. of the Senate
Recd. December 28, 1839—12 o'clock
Wm. G. Lewis Private Secretary[54]

Persons of admixture of African blood had practically no rights and privileges in Texas. The following petition will verify this statement:

To the Honorable Congress of Texas

The petition of Samuel McCulloch, Jr. of Jackson County respectfully represents that he emigrated from the United States to Texas in the family of his father, Samuel McCulloch the older, also of Jackson County, in the spring of the year of 1835, being then a single man. That when the Revolution commenced he entered the military service of Texas as a private in the Matagorda Volunteer Company commanded by Captain James Collingsworth, and under his command he participated in the storming of the Fort at Goliad on the 9th of October, 1835. In that action he received a severe wound in the right shoulder which laid him up a helpless invalid for nearly a year and has made him a cripple for life. He was the only one of the Texas Troop wounded in that action and the first whose blood was shed in the War for Independence.

He was a citizen of Texas while Texas was a part of the Republic of Mexico and was entitled to lands as a settler, but was turned down on his claim by the Mexican government and deprived the privilege of citizenship by the Republic of Texas on account of admixture of African blood.[55]

This above petition was refused by the Congress of Texas for the sole reason of admixture of African blood, as such persons were not permitted to hold land or settle in the Republic of Texas.

For the laws pertaining to slaves during the Republic of Texas, the reader is referred to the Appendix.

Chapter IV
Annexation and the Slavery Question

Attempts of United States to Acquire Texas; Opinion of American Statesmen on the Question of Slavery and Annexation; Border Raids between Louisiana and Texas; Texas Rejection of Annexation; British Plan of Abolition of Slaves in America; The South In Favor of Annexation of Texas; President Jones' Valedictory Address

The obtaining of Texas had been a problem with the United States for approximately twenty-five years before the annexation took place. As far back as 1819, John Quincy Adams had endeavored to secure a boundary which would include Texas, It was this attempt of the United States to purchase the territory between the Sabine River and the Rio Grande that served to alarm Mexico. The several offers of the United States in regard to the acquisition of Texas may be included as one of the causes of "The Decree of April 6, 1830" by Mexico.[56]

The United States was anxious to possess Texas for several reasons:
1. The acquisition of Texas fell in line with her general expansion movement.
2. The attractions of the Texas region; here were river lands for cotton and the prairies for cattle.
3. The establishment of balance of power in Congress.

The South at this time was in minority in both Houses of Congress and was very anxious to see Texas annexed, not for the purpose of power to encroach upon the North, but to protect and defend themselves. The South argued that if the balance of power was once established, the abolitionists would then let them alone, and the blighting agitation of freeing the slaves would die its natural death. The South also calculated that Texas, due to its peculiarly good soil and salubrious climate, would be a safe and convenient place for a slave population.

Mr. Calhoun avowed his opinions in the Senate of the United States as early as May 23, 1836: "There were powerful reasons why Texas should be a part of this Union. The Southern states, owning a slave population, were deeply interested in preventing that country from having the power to annoy them; and the navigating and manufacturing interests of the North, were equally interested in making it a part of the Union."[57]

The Cuban slave-trade had fearfully increased during this period, and fresh commissions were constantly arriving at Havana from Texas to buy the wretched sons of Africa who had been torn from their native soil, and transplanted across the ocean by fiends in human shape.

The project of annexation was not suffered to sleep, and the great end, too, which it would eventually subserve, was kept distinctly in view. The American Statesmen realized that the establishment, in the very midst of their slave-holding states, of an independent government by a people born and reared for the most part in the United States could not fail to produce the most unhappy effects upon both parties. For Texas would afford a ready refuge for the fugitive slaves of Louisiana and Arkansas, and would hold out an encouragement to run-away slaves, which no legislative regulations of those states could possibly counteract.

Frequent border raids and wars on account of fugitive slaves occurred between Texas and Louisiana, and these raids and wars were not only annoying and irritating, but also very expensive. Border wars over slave-property between Texas and Louisiana were not uncommon from 1840-1845. Overseers would run slaves to Texas and sell or work them. Negroes at times would kill their masters and then escape as fugitives across the border.

A leading paper states, "Annexation is desired for the purpose of sustaining and extending the institution of slavery."[58] Mr. Calhoun declared, "That what is called slavery, is in reality a political institution; essential to the peace, safety, and prosperity of those States in the Union in which it exists."[59]

When Texas gained her independence in the year of 1836, the question of annexation immediately became an issue with her citizens. The settlers of Texas were almost unanimously in favor of annexation. Stephen Fuller Austin, the leader of the United States' citizens in Texas, had in 1830 put himself on record as definitely opposed to the acquisition of Texas by the United States, but had now changed his opinion.[60]

Austin's colony constituted the predominant element of the Anglo-Americans in Texas, and he was the foremost figure among them, but it is very probable, however, that the appearance of Houston accentuated, if it did not initiate, the movement for annexation. The attempts to enforce the law that had been passed in 1830 as a result of Alaman's recommendation to the Congress of Mexico, had antagonized the people from the United States who were in Texas, and they now longed for the shelter and protection of the United States.

But the United States hesitated when the question of annexation was broached, and finally rejected the solicitations of the Republic of Texas. The reply, as recorded, reads:

The question of the annexation of a foreign independent State to the United States has never before been presented to this government. Since the adoption of their constitution, two large additions have been made to the domain originally claimed by the United States. In acquiring them, this government was not actuated by a mere thirst for sway over a broader space. Paramount interests of many of the confederacy, and the permanent well-being of all, imperatively urged upon this government the necessity of an extension of its jurisdiction over Louisiana and Florida. As peace, however, was our cherished policy, never to be departed from unless honor should be imperilled by adhering to it, we patiently endured for a time serious inconveniences and privations, and sought a transfer of those regions by negotiations and not by conquest.

The issue of those negotiations was a conditional cession of these countries to the United States. The circumstance, however, of their being colonial possessions of France and Spain, and therefore dependent on the metropolitan Governments, renders those transactions materially different from that which would be presented by the question of the annexation of Texas. The latter is a state with an independent Government, acknowledged as such by the United States, and claiming a territory beyond, though bordering on the region ceded by France, in the treaty of the 30th of April, 1803. Whether the Constitution of the United States contemplated the annexation of such a State, and if so, in what manner that object is to be effected, are questions, in the opinion of the President, it would be inexpedient, under existing circumstances, to agitate.

So long as Texas shall remain at war, while the United States are at peace with her adversary, the proposition of the Texas minister plenipotentiary necessarily involves the question of war with that adversary. The United States are bound to Mexico by a treaty of amity and commerce, which will be scrupulously observed on their part, so long as it can be reasonably hoped that Mexico will perform her duties and respect our rights under it. The United States might justly be suspected of a disregard of the friendly purposes of the compact, if the overtures of General Hunt were to be even reserved for future consideration, as this would imply a disposition wholly at variance with the spirit of the treaty, with the uniform policy and the obvious welfare of the United States.[61]

The rejection of the solicitation was due to the presentation of so many petitions against Texas from the Northeastern States.

However, the agitation for re-annexation of Texas was kept up by the South. The question of Texas was considered by many of our statesmen as one of reannexation in view of the fact that Texas was considered part of the Louisiana Territory purchased by Thomas Jefferson in 1803. The people of the United States began to fear that England would use her influence in Texas. England was working for and desired universal emancipation of slaves, and it was thought that she was anxious to uproot slavery in Texas. The abolition of slavery in Texas would be preliminary to that of abolishing slaves in the United States. This plan of the British was not merely one of Philanthropy but the British wished the abolition of slavery in America because of her interest in the culture of sugar and cotton, in which there existed a rivalry between the United States and the British West Indies. British statesmen saw the advantages which the production of cotton in America by slave labor gave to American manufacturers and the large profits which this staple afforded to American shipping. There is no doubt that the British government greatly desired the abolition of slavery in Texas as a part of their general policy to advance their colonial and commercial interests. The British government also hoped that abolition in Texas would lead to abolition of slavery in the United States.

While Ashbel Smith was in London, it was revealed in a letter from him to Van Zandt, the Texan Charge at Washington, that it was the purpose of England to procure the abolition of slavery in Texas.

They proposed to accomplish this end by friendly negotiation and concession. The conditions contemplated were a guarantee by Great Britain of the Independence of Texas; discriminating duties in favor of Texan products, and a negotiation of a loan by which the finances of Texas could be readjusted. They estimated the number of slaves at 12,000, and considered the payment for them in full as a small sum for the establishment of a free State on the Southern borders of the slave-holding States of the American Union.[62]

The abolitionists of the North, and a few in the South, opposed the annexation of Texas because more slave-territory would be added to the United States.

Calhoun, the champion of the South for the annexation of Texas, argued that the abolitionists were allies of England and enemies of their own country. "If the negroes are emancipated, the South will no longer be able to buy the productions of the North, and the North and South will be involved in common ruin."[63]

South Carolina, through Calhoun, declared, "To our section, the present issue is a question of absolute self-preservation; so much so, that it were infinitely better for us to abandon the Union, than to give up Texas to become a colony of Great Britain."[64]

General Hamilton, a well known citizen of the United States, wrote, that "If Texas slave-holders are not fit for admission into the Union, I and my fellow citizens are not fit to be there".[65]

A Civil War even then threatened in South Carolina, and in an editorial of the *Washington Spectator* it was declared, "In the Union, or out of the Union, Texas shall be our."[66]

The South feared that England might use Texas as the means of bringing about abolition in the United States, because an anti-slavery Texas dominated by England and an anti-slavery North would be a menace to slavery in the South.

It was feared that the refusal of annexation of Texas might bring on one of three results:
1. The South and Southwest might unite with Texas;
2. The tariff might be abolished;
3. Vast smuggling operations might virtually nullify the tariff, destroy our revenue, demoralize our people, and make direct taxation inevitable.

An annexation treaty was considered the most effectual, if not the only means of guarding against the threatened danger, and securing the permanent peace of the United States.

To refuse Texas annexation would be to produce a hostile feeling there, and she would go over to the old enemy of the United States. A mutually advantageous arrangement between her and England would be the consequence. All told, Texas cotton planters would have an advantage of twenty per cent over those of the Southern states of the United States. The staple would cease to be raised on the plantations of the United States and the North and West would lose their market. Texas was selling her cotton free of duty to England, and received England's manufactures without a tariff. There would be a strong inducement for the South and Southwest to unite with Texas and thus secure the same market free of duty for their cotton, and receive the same cheap manufactures, free of duty in exchange. Moreover, the slave states, if thus associated, would build up cities of their own, whereas, then they were building up New York.

Texas, if a free state, would be a haven for run-away slaves and would cause friction with the Southern states.

These were the arguments in favor of annexation of Texas from the South and from the North, until annexation was effected in 1846.

President Jones of the Republic of Texas in his valedictory in February, 1846, said:

> Gentlemen of the Senate and the House of Representative,
> The great measure of annexation so earnestly desired by the people of Texas, is happily consummated.
> The Lone Star of Texas, which ten years since arose amid clouds over fields of carnage and obscurely shone for a while, has culminated, and, following an inscrutable destiny, has passed on and become fixed forever in that glorious constellation which all freemen and lovers of freedom in the world must reverence and adore, the American Union. The final act in this great drama is now performed—the Republic of Texas is no more.[67]

Upon the annexation of Texas to the United States, war was declared between Mexico and our country in May, 1846.

The relations of cause and effect hold true in the moral as sure as in the material world. Nations reap what they sow. The treatment of both the red and the black man, had habituated us to feel our power and forget right.

The main-spring of the war between Mexico and the United States was the question of slavery. The scheme of annexation was devised, and openly declared by some of the staunchest advocates, to give greater security to the institutions of the South. The clear and direct inference is, that slavery and the war with Mexico have had a cause-and-effect connection. Had slavery not existed in our land, there would have been no annexation; had there been no annexation, there would have been no strife with Mexico.

Chapter V
Texas Plantations

Distribution of Plantations; Location and Description of Old Plantations; Life on the Plantation; Plantation Rules; Daily Occupation Record; Record of Cotton Picking; Daily Routine of Slaves

A plantation was a unit in the agricultural industry in which the laboring force was of considerable size. The work was divided among groups of laborers who worked in routine under supervision.

The primary purpose was in each case the production of a special staple commodity for sale. The laborers were generally in a status of bondage.

Cotton was the one product of the plantation that had the great virtue of keeping the laborers busy nearly all the year in a steady routine. No time of fair weather at any season needed be lost in that idleness and unenumerative work which it was the planters' chief business to guard against.

The deep and durable soils of the Brazos, Trinity, and Colorado bottoms were well adapted to the use of large numbers of slaves in raising cotton.

The influence of the plantation system and problems was local and lasting. The system gave a tone of authority and paternalism to the master class, and of obedience to the servants. The plantation problems were those of the whole community, and later became, and still are, the negro problem.

In Texas, the plantations were sparsely distributed and industry was somewhat diversified. The proportion of negro slaves was smaller than in other Southern states. The oldest plantations were in Austin's colony, and in the present counties of Brazoria and Wharton were best known of these plantations. Peach Point, which was the home of Mrs. James F. Perry, a sister of Stephen F. Austin, was located in the southern part of Brazoria County.

The Munson, Lawwood, and Ellersly plantations were all three on the Gulf prairies; they were established for producing the staple crops of cotton and sugar cane. The Lawwood plantation was developed by brothers, Robert and David G. Mills, while the Ellersly plantation was developed by J. Greenville McNeel.

The plantation named *Pleasant Grove* was that of Leander McNeel, a brother of J. Greenville McNeel, and joined the plantation of the latter on the North. The Pleasant Grove plantation had established on it a beautiful home, marble mantels and hearths and was two-story; it was elegantly furnished throughout. The cabins for the slaves were built of brick, and so was the sugar house.

Christopher Bell owned and cultivated a large plantation near the Bernard River and the Caney Bottom; the latter is still famous and frequented for its hunting grounds for large game, such as bear and deer, and occasionally a panther.

Colonel Fannin, who lost his life in the Goliad Massacre, owned jointly with Charles Mims, a plantation in Brazoria County.

Near the edge of the present town of Brazoria, was located the Spencer plantation. Mansur, the son-in-law of Spencer, peddled his negroes in Texas at anything he could get for them when he became convinced that the South would lose the war.

The Masterson plantation was another well equipped one and the ruins of former habitation can still be seen.[68]

The old Jackson plantation was located in the tropical

wilderness of Brazoria County where bullfrogs bellow and wild grape vines are tangled among the live oaks. At one end of an almost hidden crescent lake stand the ruins of an old red brick mansion with tall ivy-colored walls. This is the pathetic remnant of the stately residence fashioned by crews of sweating black men nearly 100 years ago.

In the early days of Austin's Colony this land belonged to Patrick C. and William H. Jack. In 1843 it was bought by Major Abner Jackson from Georgia who moved with his family to Texas. Major Jackson possessed a great fortune and many slaves. Among his slaves were expert brick masons, and these erected in a short time all the necessary buildings of the large plantation. Four miles of water front along the Brazos River and considerable land along Oyster Creek were included in this plantation.

The mansion was a twelve-room colonial building; six long galleries were supported by huge brick columns. It was furnished in the greatest elegance, and, although built by slave labor, it cost $35,000. This handsome residence, sugar house, and extensive negro quarters were built of home-made brick and covered by a thick coating of cement.

Brick walls surrounded extensive orchards and gardens. An island was built by slaves in the lake opposite the side door of the mansion.

One of the most stupendous tasks ever attempted in South Texas was that of digging a canal about a mile long by the Jackson slaves. Major Jackson, in 1847, conceived this idea of excavating a steamboat canal to connect Oyster Creek with Bastrop Bayou. A clearing was made and log cabins were built in the section known as *Canal Bottom*. Although the plantation was running full force, Major Jackson kept from fifty to seventy-five slaves constantly at work on the canal. As a rule, negroes are not easily affected by malaria, but in this instance, so many of the slaves succumbed to this disease that the negroes claimed that the dying slaves put a "kunjur" on Lake Jackson property.

At the beginning of the war between the states, Major Jackson owned four hundred slaves and three sugar plantations embracing 70,000 acres of land. They were the most highly developed property in Brazoria County. Steamboats halted on the river at the Jackson Landing, while crews of chanting negroes loaded cotton, sugar, and molasses. For years a tramway connected the landing with the sugar house.[69]

Plantation life had its pleasures and a degree of elegance. There were well trained house servants that treaded softly the stately rooms, and negro coachmen in livery drove planters' carriages. When the great plantation bell tolled at sunrise, squads of workers streamed from the quarters to the fields. With nightfall, banjos tinkled and flat feet shuffled. Black women crooned to their babies and admonished the older children, "Don' go clos' to de water or dat ol' debbil alligator'll snap off bofe yo' laigs..."[70]

The general description of a Texas plantation might be given as a large tract of land with a manor house on a suitable location on the plantation and cabins for the occupancy of the slaves.

The quarters for the slaves usually lined the approach-road and were log cabins about thirty feet long and twenty feet wide; an eight feet wall with a high loft and shingle roof. Each, divided in the middle and having a brick or rock chimney outside the wall at each end, was intended to be occupied by two families. The price of erecting a negro cabin was usually less than $200.

The house servants were neatly dressed, but the field hands wore very coarse and ragged garments.

The management of the slaves was usually left to overseers whose salaries ranged from $30 to $600 per month. However, definite rules and regulations for the management of the slaves were given out by the master of the slaves.

Tait's plantation was near Columbus in Colorado County, and from the original records is given the following data:

Plantation Rules
General Rules

1. Never punish a negro when in a passion. No one is capable of properly regulating the punishment for an offense when angry.
2. Never require of a negro what is unreasonable. But when you give an order be sure to enforce it with firmness, yet mildly;
3. Always attempt to govern by reason in the first instance, and resort to force only when reason fails, and then use no more force than is absolutely necessary to procure obedience.
4. In giving orders always do it in a mild tone and try to leave the impression on the mind of the negro that what you say is the result of reflection.
5. In giving orders be sure that you are understood, and let the negro know that he can always ask for an explanation if he does not understand you.
6. When you are under the necessity of punishing a negro, be sure and let him know for what offense he is punished.
7. Never act in such a way as to leave the impression on the mind of the negro that you take pleasure in his punishment; your manner should indicate that his punishment is painful.
8. A regular and systematic plan of operation is

greatly promotive of easy government. Have all matters therefore as far as possible reduced to system.
9. Negroes lack the motive of self-interest to make them careful and diligent, hence the necessity of great patience in the management of them. Do not notice therefore too many small omissions of duty.
10. The maxim of making haste slow in plantation operations is equally applicable as in ordinary vocations of life. The meaning of which is not by attempting to do too much to over-work and consequently injure your hands. Recollect that the journey of life is a long and at best a tedious one. The traveler who wishes to make a long and safe trip, always travels in regular and moderate stages. Do not kill the goose to obtain the golden egg.[71]

Particular Rules

1. Always require the negroes to eat their breakfast before they go to work.
2. From the first of October to the first of April they must be ready to go to work at daylight, stopping at 1M. long enough to eat their dinner, or as long as one hour according to circumstances.
3. From the first of April to the first of October they must be ready to go to work at sunrise, stopping at 12 M. and eating from one to two hours and a half according to circumstances.
4. Never require field-work of a woman until the expiration of four weeks after confinement and then permit her to come home to her child be-

tween breakfast and dinner, at dinner, and between dinner and night until the child is seven months old, and after that, once a day until the child is a year old or weaned.

5. Serve to every working hand once a week from two and a half to three and a half pounds of bacon according to circumstances. If milk and butter is plenty, then less meat; if molasses is served out, then one quart in place of one pound of meat. Of dried beef five or six pounds is the weekly allowance, also one peck of meal. When potatoes are served then less meal. Lying-in women to be allowed one quart of coffee and two pounds of sugar and fed from the overseers kitchen two weeks.
6. The negroes are to be allowed to commence using the potatoes and sugar cane on the first of October.
7. In clearing land, always cut and belt the timber within one foot of the ground; and cut down as much timber as can be got rid of.
8. In making rails, get them ten feet long and never heart a tree that is less than a foot in diameter; always pile the rails on the stump of the tree before leaving.
9. In making fences, lay the worm four feet and a half wide; make it five feet high and then stake with Post-Oak or Milberry rails well set in with a heavy rider.
10. Pork-hogs are to be penned in September and fed on corn previously shelled and soaked in water two or three days. Pumpkins, sugar-cane etc.
11. In planting corn, mix pumpkin seeds with the corn for every fourth row.

12. Potatoes when dug to be housed or banked the same day.
13. The women to commence in November spinning thread at night to make plow lines.
14. The corn to be gathered as soon as it is dry enough.
15. No profane or obscene language to be allowed among the negroes.
16. Every negro cabin to be inspected every Sunday morning to see that it is kept clean. Every negro to appear in the field on Monday morning in clean clothes.
17. The negroes are never to be allowed to leave the premises, unless by special permission and a written paper stating where they are permitted to go.
18. No strange negro to be allowed to visit the plantation, unless by permission of the overseer, and a written paper from his master.
19. Every overseer on taking charge of the plantation, is to take an inventory of the effects then on the place and to do the same before leaving.[72]

From an original document the following extract is given with the spelling, punctuation, and form of the original document retained as nearly as possible:

Journal kept by Stephen S. Perry during the year 1848:

Month & Day	Occupation	Delinquency
January 16	Gin is running Making rails thering down and rebuilding fences	Allin sick
17	Making fences, Cleaning the gutters,	Allin sick

18	Shelling Corn Gin running Tearing down and rebuilding fences. Cut down the hedge in the Prairie field. Making rails Gin running until 9 oc at night	Bill sick 1 Allin sick 1
19	Taring down and rebuilding fences	Ben and Chaney sick 1 Allin sick 1
20	Taring down and rebuilding fences	Allin Sick 1
21	Finished rebuilding fences in the Prairie field	Allin sick 1
22	Sunday	Allin Sick 1
23	Making cotton bailes (made 16) carryin Cotton into gin house	Allin sick 1
24	Weighing cotton bailes, shelling corn	Allin sick 1
25	Making Ben's chimley	Allen sick 1
26	Finished Ben's chimley. Commenced rebuilding fence in the Bottom field	Allin sick Mary and Ben sick
27	Killed fifteen Hogs. Cut them up and salted, part of the hands was occupied carrying cotton from the pens into the Gin hous. Gin running	Mary and Ben and Allin sick Bill sick half a day
28	Killed ten hogs Cut them up and salted, part of the hands occupied carrying cotton from the pens to the Gin hous. Gin running	Allin sick
29	Shelling corn All hands continued building fences	Allin sick
30	Sunday	Allin sick
31	Taring down and rebuilding fences. Hunting sowes and pigs, put nine sowes with forty young pigs in the Prairie field	Allin sick
February 1	Killed sixteen hogs this morning cut them and salted, continue making fence	Allin sick George sick
2	Making fence and splitting rails Shiped to Aycock's landing fifteen sacks of corn containing 40 bushels to be sent to Judge Law Galveston	George sick Allin sick

3	Making and splitting railes, continue building fence	Allin sick
4	Making cotton bailes, made fifteen bailes carrying cotton in to the Gin	Allin sick
5	Continued to bail Made seven bailes weighed and shipped eleven to Mr. Aycock's Landing Making fence gin stoped today	Allin sick
6	Sunday	
7	Finished building the back string of fence in the Bottom field Shiped eleven bailes of Cotton to the Aycock Landing	Allin and Mary sick
8	Commenced pulling cotton stocks and cleaning the corn ground	Allin and Mary sick
9	Continued to pull and roll Cotton Stocks and cleaning up corn ground	
10	Ploughs commenced today the 9 of Feb.	
11	Three ploughs running, cleaning up Cotton Stocks	
12	Ploughing and cleaning up ground	
13	Ploughing	
14	Ploughing	
15	Ploughing and braking down Cotton stocks	Betty sick this afternoon George absent today Silvey working in the garden
16	Ploughing finished gining today	
17	Ploughing and braking down cotton stocks	Becky started working in the field today stoped working in the field

Jan. 3

From another extract of an Original Document in the Texas Library at Austin, Texas:

Delinquences during the months from the 17 January to the first of April:

	Number of days sick
Allin	24
Bill	Day and one half
Silvey	sick 1
George	sick 3
May Ben	sick 4
Ben	sick 3
Tom	sick 3
Clennen	sick 2
Mary Ann	sick 11
John	sick 9
Peter	sick 2
Bob	sick 1

Silvey absent from the field. Days working at the house

	Days
Silvey	11
George absent	4
Becky working at the house	14
Wesley absent	1

From the Peach Point Plantation is taken the following specimen page of cotton picking record:[73]

68   Slavery in Texas

1845 August	5	6	7	8	9	11	12	13	14
Allin	140	63	107			107	138	117	140
Bill			155	87		257	270	248	280
Ben									194
Betcey	262	113	117	167	104	169	170	118	205
Bob	292	113	178	265	184	200	232	235	205
Becky		85	118	97	91	84	115	276	134
Clennen									164
Caroline	309	145	246	254	225	262	282		333
Chaney	125	100	191	108	161		165	190	296
Charlot	219	110	164	148	215	151	246		235
George	301		173	219	125	251		101	200
John	231		126	137	175	144	152	166	200
John Jack				166	164	224	221	235	233
Lowey	289	115	186	161	182	182	176		205
Mary		92	168		77		291		174
Ned					145		126	288	85
Peter				145		126	150	86	137
Purnell	258		140						60
Robert						263	108	25	
Silvey						142	150	110	
Westley						94			
Sam						93			

Prairie Field	242	6							4312
Fine Cotton		823							
Timbered Field		206	1940	1696	2597	2934	2579		
		6							

An accurate account was kept of the work done by each slave; this can be seen from the above extracts.

In 1848 cotton sold for three cents per pound, and this

averaged $174 as the net yield per slave.[74]

While cotton picking may be considered hard labor, it was and still is the favorite labor of the negro. A cotton picking day was not an irksome task for the slave. The big plantation bell would ring out at the first streak of dawn as the overseer had shaken off sleep.

Twinkling lights would soon be seen in the doorways of the cabins, and then the sound of the axe as wood was chopped to build the fires under long rows of umbrella trees. Then kettles hummed and hoe-cakes were prepared for breakfast.

Mules were hitched to the numbered wagons, and as the rumbling carts approached, darky women with gaily bandannaed heads hastily gathered their broods and picked up lunches and hurried to the roadside where they exchanged extravagant greetings with their friends. With much shouted advice in carnival spirit, they would pile into the wagons which went their way to join the others in a long train moving slowly down the hill to the fields. One by one the wagons forked from the main road into their allotted fields.[75]

The long white cotton sacks would soon be thrown over the shoulders, and up and down the slaves slowly wended their way with bowed backs as they gathered the cotton. At noon there was the lunch to be eaten under the shade of the trees, and the pleasant exchange of the darkies with one another.

Again they took to the field and then late in the evening, steadily sack after sack was weighed and emptied into the wagon; willing boys with savage foot-thrusts tramped the cotton so that a full bale might be packed between the high-slatted sides. As the shadows lengthened, the negroes climbed onto the wagons to loll on the soft cotton on the homeward way. After supper the negroes delighted in sitting in front of their cabins playing the banjo and chanting the old spirituals.

The slave was happy and their world on the plantation was good enough with cotton, corn, mules, and the 'possum in the woods.

Chapter VI
Slavery During Texas Statehood

Tax Collector's Receipt; Texas Slave Population; Principal Slave-Holding Counties; Sale of Slaves; Laws Regulating Slave Hiring; Manumission

When Texas was annexed in 1846, she came into the Union as a slave state with all the rights and protection of property guaranteed her citizens under the Constitution of the United States.

Slavery had existed in Texas during the time that it was under Mexican rule; it continued to exist after she had won her independence, nor did the annexation to the United States change the status of the slave in Texas. Plantations continued to thrive and the wealth of the state rapidly increased at the expense of human beings held in bondage. Slaves continued to be classed as the property of their master and as such were assessed along with other property. The following is an excerpt from the original files of the Piper Papers:

> Received of Benjamins Piper five Dollars and Eighty cents, in full for his State and County Tax due the County of Travis for the year 1849 including 6 negroes 3 horses 8 cattle 200 dollars loaned at interest, wagon
> T. B. Beck
> Assessor and Collector T.C.[76]

Another tax receipt reads:

$14.18

Received of Susan Piper the sum of Fourteen Dollars and Eighteen Cents as State and County Tax for the year 1856 on the following property situated in the County of Travis viz:
200 Acres San De Valle Tract 6 negroes 2 horses 1 wagon and Team
This 5th day of June 1857
Jas. T. M. Laurin Assessor and Tax Collector
Travis County.[77]

Texas was, and remained altogether, an agricultural state and the slave population increased rapidly. The taxation figures in the State Comptroller's reports offer this basis for study:[78]

Texas Slave Population 1847-1861

Year	Number of Slaves	Total Value	Av. Value
1846	32,164	10,488,548	$326.00
1847	37,106	12,131,268	327
1848	40,610	13,398,490	330
1849	38,207	12,773,540	334
1850	48,287	17,492,500	362
1851	51,064	20,492,250	401
1852	62,797	35,946,473	456
1853	78,713	46,501,840	513
1854	90,612	53,422,663	505
1855	105,704	58,389,400	513
1856	113,736	67,497,306	539
1857	125,240	72,855,928	538
1858	135,320	85,630,833	625
1859	136,855	106,688,920	672
1860	158,595	93,848,680	403
1861	232,534		

The tax officials in 1860 assessed the 158,595 negroes at $106,688,920, which was more than 36 per cent of all property reported in Texas, $294,315,659. The next year the slave valuation decreased (sic) to $256,784,432; although there were more slaves. By 1860 Texas had a slave population of 182,566 held by 21,878 owners of whom 3,349 owned fifteen or more slaves, and only 141 planters possessed more than 100 slaves.[79]

The following table compiled from the Seventh and Eighth Census of Agriculture of the United States gives an account of the distribution as to the number of slaves owned by slave-holders in 1850 as compared to the year 1860:

Slave-holders in Texas

1850		1860	
1 slave	1935	1 slave	4593
2 and under 5	2640	2 slaves	2874
5 to 10	1585	3 slaves	2093
10 to 20	1121	4 slaves	1782
20 to 50	374	5 slaves	1439
50 to 100	82	6 slaves	1125
		7 slaves	928
		8 slaves	790
		9 slaves	668
		10 to 15 slaves	2237
		15 to 20 slaves	1186
		20 to 30 slaves	1095
		30 to 40 slaves	491
		40 to 50 slaves	241
		50 to 70 slaves	194
		70 to 100	88
		100 to 200	52
		200 to 300	2
TOTAL	7747	TOTAL	21878

The Southern and Eastern part remained the principal slave-holding regions of Texas. The assessment rolls for 1862 give this information:[80]

Name of County	Number of Slaves
Cass	4697
Harrison	8768
Austin	4226
Brazoria	7543
McCellan	2366
Bee	132
Kerr	47
Bexar	28

The free colored people in Texas were distributed irregularly according to the figures given by the census of Texas in 1858:

Name of County	Number of Free Colored Persons
Austin	12
Brazoria	5
Erath	13
Harris	28
Matagorda	1

Until passage of an Act of January 27, 1858, authorizing free negroes to choose masters, the laws of Texas did not recognize any persons as slaves except such as were the offspring of slave-mothers.

No negro could sell himself into slavery. In this respect, the Institution of Slavery in Texas differed widely from that of Rome. Slavery under the Roman law might originate in three ways, namely: by birth, when the mother was a slave; by captivity in war; and by the voluntary sale of himself by a freeman.

The chief agricultural products of Texas remained cotton and sugar. The largest cotton counties in 1858 were:

Name of County	Number of Acres
Harrison	51708
Washington	28886
Rusk	25780
Austin	20464
Cass	20168
Fayette	18723
Grimes	18316
Upshur	16692
Gonzales	16193
Colorado	15863
Cherokee	15374
Wharton	13094
Polk	12270
Nacogdoches	11823

The following were the largest sugar counties:[81]

Name of County	Number of Acres
Brazoria	7187
Matagorda	1160
Fort Bend	690
Washington	417

To give the reader an idea of the wealth in Texas, the following table will be of interest:

Assessments in Austin County for 1859
S, Brewer, Tax Assessor and Collector

314,188 Acres of Land valued at	$1,560,979	at 12% on $100	$195,122
193 Town Lots valued at	$81,800	at 12%	$10,225
2,745 Negroes valued at	$1,548,800	at 12%	$193,600
3,737 Horses valued at	$199,275	at 12%	$24,909
37,728 Cattle valued at	$230,391	at 12%	$28,799
37 Money Lenders Amount	$64,441	at 20%	$12,888
Miscellaneous	$91,842	at 12%	$11,481
TOTAL VALUE	$3,777,531	Ad Valorem Tax	$477,024
		Poll Tax	$37,950.00

The average value of property assessed was:[82]

Land	$4,96 per acre
Lots	429.00
Negroes	564.22
Horses	53.32
Cattle	6.10

Slaves were bought and sold as during the Republic:[83]

The State of Texas County of Travis

Know all men by these presents that Rebecca Carolina Thompson of said state and county for and in consideration of the sum or Five Hundred and Thirty Dollars to me in hand paid by Benjamins Piper of the same place, the receipt whereof is hereby acknowledged, have this day bargained, sold, and delivered unto him the said Piper, one certain Negro Boy named Bob, the same willed and bequeathed to me by My father Godson White, and I do hereby forever relinquish the right and ownership over said boy, Bob, to the said Piper, his

heirs and assigns and I will forever warrant and defend the title of said Piper and his heirs.
In testimony whereof I here unto sign my name and affix my seal this March 13, 1849
Rebecca C. Thompson

The State of Texas County of Travis

Personally came before me Rebecca C. Thompson, and acknowledged that she signed the foregoing bill of sale for the purposes and considerations therein expressed.
Given under my hand and seal of office at Austin March 13, 1849
H. E. McCulloch
NOTARY PUBLIC

The state of slavery in this country compared with the Roman law in many respects. The progress of civilization and that of society, more correct notions on the subject of moral obligation, and above all, the benign influence of the Christian religion, softened many of the rigors attended upon slavery among the ancients. But the rights of the slave in regard to marriage and the acquisition of property by way of inheritance remained substantially on the same ground.

Slaves could not marry, even with the consent of their masters, so as to constitute them husband and wife and protect them from being witnesses against each other. They could not take property by purchase or descent. They had no heirs and could not make a will. They were not entitled to the rights and considerations of matrimony, therefore there was no relief in cases of adultery.

The confession of a slave was not evidence in a suit against the master, on a contract of hiring, or for injury caused by the wrongful act of a slave. Negro testimony was inadmissible in all cases, except for and against each other.

The following cases are cited:

> Ingram and wife v. Linn Administrator
> Whereas the petition alleged that the slave of the defendant persuaded, decoyed, and enticed away the slave of the plaintiff's and forced him into the Guadalupe River, by reason of which he was drowned.[84]

The court held that the defendant was not liable.

The rule of the common law in respects to liability of the master for the tortuous acts of his servants was applicable here to the relation of master and slave. The master was answerable for the misconduct and negligence of his slave while acting in the immediate employment of the master or under his authority; but he was not answerable for a willful and unauthorized trespass committed by the slave.

> The hirer of a slave is bound to observe towards the slave the same care which a discreet, humane and prudent master would observe in the treatment of his own slaves. Less than ordinary care and diligence would render him responsible for any loss or injury which might accrue to the owner.[85]

The hirer of the slave, not the owner, was responsible for medical attendance, where the attendance was not requested by the owner, and where there was no special agreement. A slave that was hired out could not be taken in execution for a debt of the owner, where the lien had not attached before the transfer of the possession by hiring.[86]

The hirer was responsible for the slave where a written contract was made for the return of the slave. The hirer was also responsible for the loss of the slave. The measure of damage was, in general, that which would compensate the owner of the slave as nearly as possible for the actual injury sustained by the breach of contract by the defendant.[87]

A testator could, by will, emancipate his slaves, if provision was made for their removal from the state. There could not be an implied manumission of a slave. The bequest of property to a slave could not effect his emancipation. Manumission to take effect within the state was contrary to its laws and public policy which prohibited the introduction or residence of free negroes within its limits. The intent of the testator had to be ascertained from the meaning of the words in the instrument, and from these words alone.

As early as 1859, war clouds began to gather and the fate of the South and its institution of slavery was doomed before many years passed.

Chapter VII
The Emancipation of Slaves in Texas

Anti-Slavery Societies; The Work of Abolitionists; Texas' Withdrawal from the Union; Declaration of Causes of Secession; President Lincoln's Call for Volunteers; Texas' Part in the Civil War; Life on the Plantations During the Civil War; Traffic in Slaves Continues during the War; Downfall of the Southern Confederacy; General Gordon's Entry into Texas; Celebration of "Juneteenth"; Reconstruction Ordeals; The Negro and His Place in the South

The first American Anti-Slavery Society was formed at a called convention in Philadelphia in December, 1833. The object of this Society was the entire abolition of Slavery in the United States. While it admitted that each State, in which Slavery existed, had by the Constitution of the United States the exclusive right to legislate in regard to its abolition in said State, it aimed to convince people that slaveholding was a heinous crime in the sight of God.

The abolition movement spread until it reached Texas. There were but few abolitionists in Texas, but abolitionists from the North formed plots to stir up the negroes. Abolition Societies employed men to come to Texas under the pretense of securing employment or as investors. The real object of these men was to excite the negroes and to secretly provide them with ammunition and poison to use against their masters. The negroes' minds were poisoned against their masters and they were encouraged by the Abolitionists to use force to gain their freedom.

Whenever plots were detected by the owners of slaves, lynchings would take place.

By consulting the newspapers published in 1860, the following accounts were found:

> At Athens, Henderson County, a well was discovered to be poisoned on Sunday the 5th inst., and over 100 bottles of strychnine were found in possession of negroes. On examination the plot was brought to light, which was to poison as many as possible at breakfast and then the knife and the pistol, with which they were well supplied, were to do the balance of the work. All the old women and the young children were to be murdered and the young women were to be taken as wives by the hell hounds.
>
> A patrol of 100 men is on duty every night in Tyler, and this has thus far saved that town.
>
> A negro belonging to Mr. Barron at Science Hill, Henderson County, was hung on the 3rd, strychnine having been found in his possession, and he having confessed to having a hand in the insurrection.[88]

The Houston Telegraph of August 28, 1861, gives the following item: "A straggler, suspected of Abolitionism, found tampering with some negroes, was arrested at Navasota on Friday last and placed in safe keeping for examination."

The town of Henderson was burned on August 5th, 1860. Many reports of incendiary fires, poisoning, negro uprisings, and the like, which produced a mania of suspicion, leading to the expulsion of suspects and in a few cases to lynching. There sprang into existence Committees of Safety, military companies, and the organization of the K.G.C. found a ready welcome. The latter was the organization of the Knights of the Golden Circle which was similar to that of the Ku Klux Klan organized during the

Reconstruction Period of the South and whose members sympathized with the slave-holders.

The State Gazette of Austin, Texas, December 8, 1860, published the following article:

> To Our Fellow Citizens of the State of Texas
> The election of a president of the United States by the great sectional party of the North has been accomplished.
> The insults, threats, and aggressions which have been directed at the honor, the equality, and the happy social existence of the people of Texas and the South for the last forty years have reached a climax.
> The people of Texas are justly alarmed at the impending destruction of all that is valuable to freemen.
> The distinguished governor of our State has been petitioned by a large number of the citizens of Texas to convene her legislature, preliminary to a convention of the people."

Texas was the seventh State to withdraw from the Union. There was no other state, if we except those immediately contiguous to the free States, that had so many obstacles to contend with in the consummation of that measure. In the first place, her population was made up of emigrants, from many nations, many of whom had not been here long enough to become acquainted with our peculiar form of government, or to become assimilated in their habits of thinking and their customs.

The opposition of the Governor, who in the absence of the Legislature controlled the State government, refused to call the Legislature together.

The Governor refused to call the representatives of the people together, and this compelled them to have recourse to the extraordinary alternative of calling a convention without the aid of the government and by their own spontaneous action. The sentiment was universal that some action was absolutely necessary for the common safety. So it happened that the people of Texas, by common consent, determined that their own destinies should be controlled by themselves, and not by any one man.

Mass meetings were held in Brazoria, Walker, and some other counties, recommending a convention in Galveston; but soon after this, the people of Austin, Houston, and Galveston respectively, almost simultaneously proposed the same place, Austin. A convention was called under a uniform plan by nearly all the counties of Texas. The election of delegates to the Convention was regularly conducted in nearly all the organized Counties, and the aggregate for secession candidates, as counted by the Convention, was over 32,000; this was more than half the largest vote ever polled at any election in the State. In some two or three counties no election was held. There were fifteen anti-secession delegates to one hundred sixty secession delegates in the Convention.

The Convention met at Austin on the 28th of January. The Ordinance of Secession was prepared and carried on the fourth day of the session, the first day of February, by 167 ayes to 7 nays. The Ordinance provided the final separation of Texas from the Union should take place on the second day of March, unless rejected by the vote of the people at an election to be held for the people to approve or reject on February the 33rd.

After the convention had been called by the spontaneous voice of the people, the Governor called the Legislature in extra session to meet one week previous to the meeting of the Convention, though he had previously refused to make such a call. After the convention met, both the Legislature and the Governor recognized it as a representative body of the people, and both the Legislature and the Executive, with all the Judges and Heads of Departments of State and other public functionaries were, by invitation, in attendance at the Convention on the passage of the Ordinance of Secession. The final vote was taken under the most imposing solemnities at precisely twelve o'clock at noon.

The second day of March was fixed upon as the day for making the solemn act of secession final, 1st, Because it was the anniversary of our separation from Mexico; 2cd, Because secession could only be postponed one day longer without subjecting Texas to "Black Republican" rule, which commenced on the fourth of March, and the people of Texas desired especially to escape the disgrace of living under Lincoln's authority even for a single day. The Convention adjourned February 5th to meet on March 2cd to count the vote of the people.

When the votes were counted, returns were received from 120 out of 123 original counties, and over 60,000 votes were polled, more than 3 to 1 of which were for secession.[89]

The Convention spent much time in amending the Constitution, and these adopted amendments are to be found in the appendix of this work and consist of laws attempting to check the Abolitionists and anyone who might aid the slaves in any uprising. These laws also provided for punishment of insurgent slaves.

The permanent Constitution of the Confederate States was adopted and ratified by a vote of 128 yeas to 1 nay. Many of the delegates had already left the Convention.

Governor Houston was deposed as governor of Texas when he declined to take the oath, of allegiance to the Confederacy. His office was declared void and Edward Clark, the Lieutenant-Governor, by virtue of existing law, became governor. Governor Houston opposed secession and firmly protested his deposition as governor, but to no avail.[90]

The Convention appointed a Committee to put into writing the causes that impelled Texas to secede from the Federal Union. This said Committee placed before the Convention the following declaration which was adopted:

> Declaration of the Causes Which Impel The State of Texas to Secede From the Federal Union:
>
> The Government of the United States by certain joint Resolutions, bearing date on the first day of March in the year A.D., 1845, proposed to the Republic of Texas, then a free, sovereign and independent nation, the annexation of the latter to the former, as one of the co-equal States of the thereof.
>
> The people of Texas, by the Deputies in Convention assembled, on the fourth of July of the same year, assented to and accepted said proposals, and formed a Constitution for the proposed State, upon which on the 29th of December, of the same year, said State was formerly received into the Confederate Union.
>
> Texas abandoned her separate national existence, and consented to become one of the Confederate States, to promote her welfare, insure domestic tranquility, and secure more substantially the blessings of liberty and peace to her people. She was received into the Confederacy with her own Constitution, under the guarantees of the Federal Constitution and the compact of annexation, that she should enjoy these blessings. She was received as a commonwealth holding, maintaining and protecting the institution known as negro-slavery — the servitude of the African to the white race within her limits; a relation that had existed from her first settlement of her wilderness by the white race, and which

her people intended should continue to exist in all future time. Her institutions and geographical position established the strongest ties between her and the other slave-holding States of the Confederacy. Those ties have been strengthened by the association. But what has been the course of the Government of the United States and of the people and authorities of the none-slave-holding States since our connection with them?

The controlling majority of the Federal Government, under various pretenses and disguises, has so administered the same as to exclude the citizens of the Southern States, unless under odious and unconstitutional restrictions, from all the immense territory owned in common by all the States on the Pacific Ocean, for the avowed purpose of acquiring sufficient power in the common government, to use it as a means of destroying the institutions of Texas and her sister slave-holding States.

By the disloyalty of the Northern States and their citizens, and the imbecility of the Federal Government, infamous combinations of incendiaries and outlaws have been permitted in those States and the common territory of Kansas, to trample upon the Federal laws and property of Southern citizens in that territory and finally, by violence and mob laws, to usurp the possession of the Northern States.

The Federal Government, while but partially under the control of our unnatural and sectional enemies, has for years almost entirely failed to protect the lives and property of the people of Texas against the Indian savages on our borders; and more recently against the murderous forays of the banditti from the neighboring territory of Mexico; and when our State Government has expended large amounts for such purposes, the Federal Government has refused reimbursement therefor, thus rendering our condition more insecure and harassing than it was during the existence of the Republic of Mexico.

These and other wrongs have been patiently borne, and in the vain hope that a returning sense of justice and humanity would induce a different course of administration.

When we advert to the course of individual slaveholding States, and that of a majority of their citizens, our grievance assume a far greater magnitude.

The States of Maine, Vermont, New Hampshire, Connecticut, Rhode Island, Massachusetts, New York, Pennsylvania, Ohio, Wisconsin, Michigan, and Iowa by solemn legislative enactments, have deliberately, directly, violated the third clause of the second section of the fourth article of the Federal Constitution, and laws passed in pursuance thereof, annulling a material provision of the compact, designed by its framers to perpetuate amity between the members of the Confederacy, and to secure the rights of the slave-holding States in their domestic institutions, a provision founded in justice and wisdom, and without the enforcement of which the compact fails to accomplish the object of its creation. Some of those States have high fines and degrading penalties upon any of their citizens or officers who may carry out in good faith that provision of the compact, or the federal laws enacted in accordance therewith.

In all the non-slaveholding States, in violation of that good faith and comity which should exist even between entirely distinct nations, the people have formed themselves into a great sectional party, now strong enough in numbers to control the affairs of each of those States, based upon the unnatural feeling of hostility to these Southern States and their beneficent and patriarchal system of African slavery, proclaiming the debasing doctrine of the equality of all men, irrespective of race or color, a doctrine at war with nature, in opposition to the experience of mankind, and in violation of the plainest revelations of the Divine law. They demand the abolition of negro slavery throughout the Confederacy, the recognition of political equality between the white and negro races, and avow their determination to press on their crusade against us, so long as a negro slave remains in these States.

For years past, this abolition organization has been actively sowing the seeds of discord through the Union, and has rendered the Federal Congress the arena for spreading fire-brands and hatred between the slaveholding and nonslaveholding States.

By consolidating their strength, they have placed the slave-holding States into a hopeless minority in the Federal Congress, and rendered representation of no avail in protecting Southern rights against their exactions and encroachments.

They have proclaimed, and at the ballot box sustained, the revolutionary doctrine that there is a "higher law" than the Constitution and laws of our Federal Union, and virtually that they disregard their oaths and trample upon our rights.

They have, for years past, encouraged and sustained lawless organizations to steal our slaves and prevent their recapture, and have repeatedly murdered Southern citizens while lawfully seeking their rendition.

They have invaded Southern soil, and murdered unoffending citizens, and through the press, their leading men and a fanatical pulpit, have bestowed praise upon the actors and assassins of these crimes, while the Governors of several of their States have refused to deliver parties implicated and indicted for participation in such offenses, upon the legal demands of the States aggrieved.

They have, through the mails and hired emissaries, sent seditious pamphlets and papers amongst us to stir up servile insurrection and bring blood and carnage to our firesides.

They have sent hired emissaries among us to burn our towns and distribute arms and poison to our slaves for the same purpose.

They have impoverished the slaveholding States by unequal and partial legislation, thereby enriching themselves by draining from us our substance.

They have refused to vote appropriations for protecting Texas against ruthless savages, for the sole reason that she is a slave-holding State.

And, finally by the combined sectional vote of the seventeen free or non-slave-holding States, they have elected as President and Vice-President of the whole Confederacy, two men whose chief claim to such high positions is their approval of these long continued wrongs, and their pledges to continue them to the final consummation of these schemes for the ruin of the slave-holding States.

In view of these and many other facts, it is meet that our own views should be distinctly proclaimed.

We hold, as undeniable truths, that the governments of various States and of the Confederacy itself, were established exclusively by the white race, for themselves and their prosperity; that the African race had no agency in their establishment; that they were rightfully held and regarded as an inferior and dependent race, and in that condition only could their existence in this country be rendered beneficial or tolerable.

That, in this free government, *all white men are, and of right ought to be, entitled to equal civil and political rights*; that the servitude of the African race, as existing in these States, is mutually beneficial to both bond and free, and is abundantly authorized and justified by the experience of mankind, and the revealed will of the Almighty Creator, as recognized by all Christian nations; while the destruction of the existing relations between the two races, as advocated by our sectional enemies, would bring inevitable calamities upon both, and desolation upon the fifteen slaveholding States.

By the secession of six of the slave-holding States, and the certainty that others will speedily do likewise, Texas has no alternative but to remain in isolated connection with the North, or unite her destinies with the South.

For these and no other reasons, solemnly asserting that the Federal Constitution has been violated and virtually abrogated by the several States named; seeing that the Federal Government is now passing under the control of our sectional enemies, to be diverted from the exalted objects of its creation, to those of oppression and wrong; and realizing that our State can no longer look for protection but to God and her sons: We, the Delegates of the people of Texas, in Convention assembled, have passed an Ordinance dissolving all political connection with the Government of the United States of America and the people thereof, and confidently appeal to the intelligence and patriotism of the freemen of Texas to ratify the same at the ballot-box on the 23rd day of the present month.

Adopted, in Convention, on the 2cd day of February, in the year of our Lord one thousand eight hundred and sixty-one, and of the Independence of Texas the twenty-fifth.[91]

The above Declaration was signed by all but six members of the Convention present.

On April 15, 1861, President Abraham Lincoln issued a proclamation for 75,000 volunteers to force the South back into the Union.[92]

Texas rallied to the cause of the South; she not only furnished more than her quota of men, but the State of Texas in the Tenth Legislature voted $10,000,000 in Confederate Treasury Notes to defray the contingent expenses.

As most men enlisted in the war, the women and children were, to a great degree, left with the slaves to take care of the plantations. From a manuscript this information was taken:

> My father owned about 75 slaves and during the war these were closely watched and housed somewhat like cattle. Cotton was the crop and the land was cultivated by means of the turning plow and the bull tongue. The land was first bedded and then logged and harrowed. After the cotton came up, it was chopped and plowed. The cotton was picked in baskets and put in rail pens. The ginning of the cotton was done by a fifty-saw gin pulled by four mules driven by two small negro boys. A larger boy put the cotton up on the gin-stand with a basket and the cotton was fed through by a grown slave (Uncle Aaron). The cotton was run into a lint box and then carried about forty yards to a compress screw press where it was tramped into a box and then tied up with a rope. The old negro's task was about two bales a day. The cotton was hauled to Houston by ox-wagon and it took from four to six weeks for a trip.[93]

The slaves, for the most part, remained loyal and protected the property and family of their masters as best they could. Only in a few instances were outbreaks of violence reported. It appears that as soon as the agitations of the Abolitionists ceased, the slave, as a rule, was fairly contented with his lot and to some degree took pride in providing and caring for the women and children who had been left at home alone.[94]

The buying and selling of slaves was by no means discarded, as indicated by this Bill of Sale:

> Know all men by these presents that. I, A. C. J. Anderson of the County of Collins and the State of Texas of the first part for and in consideration of the sum of Seventeen hundred Dollars Confederate money to me in hand paid by Nathan Anderson of the County of Hunt and State aforesaid of the second part the receipt whereof is hereby acknowledged, have bargained and sold and by this presents do bargain and sell, grant and convey unto the said party of the Second part, his executors, administrators, and assigns, One Negro boy, Frank, dark, age 30 years and a slave for life.
> To have and to hold Same unto the said party of the second part, his executors, administrators, and assigns forever.
> A. C. J. Anderson
> May 10th 1864
> Witness: Nancy C. McKinney[95]

The traffic in slaves in Texas was lawful until the final surrender of the insurgent forces and the proclamation of that fact by the commanding general. The loss fell and had to be borne by those who were the owners of slaves at the time of their liberation.[96] The courts held that although President Lincoln had declared slaves free January 1, 1863, such freedom did not exist actually until June 19, 1865, and consequently law suits over the payment for slaves were decided in the courts as cited above. In regard to the legality of notes for slaves sold, both parties had the same means of knowing the future condition of the slave and acted upon his own idea as to the results of the war.

Slaves were property, a chattel interest established by the constitution and local municipal laws of Texas, recognized by the constitution and laws of the United States, as a part of the civil polity of the State, with which the national authority had no right to interfere in the ordinary civil action of the government.

The downfall of the Southern Confederacy occurred May 25, 1865, and the United States emerged from the great military struggle with the Union preserved and slavery an institution of the past.

General Gordon Granger entered Texas and issued the order for the emancipation of slaves in Texas on June 19, 1865.[97]

It is this date that gave the negroes in Texas the joyous "Juneteenth" that is celebrated by them year after year in commemoration of their emancipation.

Texas passed through the ordeals of the Reconstruction period with the other States of the South. Such organizations as the Ku Klux Klan, Union League, Knights of the White Camelia, and the Freedman's Bureau were organized and operated until the Conservatives regained political control.[98]

In conclusion, may it be said, that the Negro in Texas has a genuine place in society. It is secondary, but it is certain.

He lives and moves and has his being in the security of a definite status. He is free in his station. However desolate his freedom, and however humble his cabin may be, he is happy. Being of a different racial type, he has a philosophy different from ours and he enjoys life, and he lives to enjoy; he was born with the capacity for its enjoyment.

In the South, where racial and social equality with the negro is sensibly rejected as monstrous, the white man continues to temper the wind for the negro. The white man in the South, understands the negro as no Northern people ever have or ever will. Hence the negro problem which has been left as an aftermath of slavery is being worked out more satisfactorily in the South than in any other section of the country.

Appendix

Slavery Laws During the Republic of Texas
Constitution of the Republic of Texas

Section 6: ...All free white persons who emigrate to the Republic, and who shall, after a residence of six months, make oath before some competent authority that he intends to reside permanently in the same, and shall swear and support this constitution, and that he will bear true allegiance to the Republic of Texas, shall be entitled to all the privileges of citizenship.

Section 9: ...All persons of color who were slaves for life previous to their emigration to Texas, and who are now held in bondage, shall remain in the like state of servitude; provided, the said slave shall be a bonafide property of the person so holding said slave as aforesaid. Congress shall pass no laws to prohibit emigrants from bringing their slaves into the Republic with them, and holding them by the same tenure by which such slaves were held in the United States; nor shall Congress have power to emancipate slaves; nor shall any slave-holder be allowed to emancipate his or her slave or slaves without the consent of Congress, unless he or she shall send his or her slave or slaves without the limit of the Republic. No free person of African descent, either in whole or in part, shall be permitted to reside permanently in the Republic without the consent of Congress; and the importation or admission of Africans or negroes into this Republic, excepting from the United States of America, is forever prohibited, and declared to be piracy.

Section 10: ...All persons (Africans, the descendants of Africans, and Indians excepted), who were residing in Texas on the day of the Declaration of Independence, shall be considered citizens of the Republic, and entitled to all the privileges of such. All citizens now living in Texas, who have not received their portion of land, in like manner as colonists, shall be entitled to their land in the following proportion and manner.[99]

Immediately upon the adoption of the Constitution, President Burnet, on April 3, 1836, issued the following proclamation:

Proclamation By The President

Whereas the ninth article of the general provisions of The Constitution of the Republic of Texas provides that the importation or admission of Africans or Negroes into this Republic, excepting from the United States of America is forever prohibited and declared to be piracy, and
Whereas, the African slave-trade is equally revolting to the best feelings of our nature and to the benign principles of the Christian faith, is equally destructive to national morals and to individual humanity; and
Whereas, the most enlightened and powerful nations of Christendom are exerting both their moral influence and physical force to suppress that odious and abominable traffic; and
Whereas, it is the imperative duty and the high privilege of the Government of Texas to contribute in all practicable and legitimate means to the effectual prevention in its own jurisdiction of a trade so atrocious and disreputable.

Therefore, I, David G. Burnet, President of the Republic of Texas, by and with the advice and consent of my Cabinet, and in accordance with the ninth article of the Constitution aforesaid, do command and require all officers, naval and military, and all collectors and other functionaries of the Government to be vigilant and active in detecting and defeating any attempt to violate said article, and to seize, and to arrest, and detain in safe custody, any person or persons that may be found violating or attempting to violate the same; and to stop, seize, take possession of and detain any vessel or vessels with their equipment, tackle, and any boat or other water craft of any description attached thereto, on board of which any Africans or Negroes so attempted to be imported in contravention of the said ninth article may be found, and to detain any and all such negroes wherever found until the further decision of the Government can be had in relation thereto; provided that any officer making such seizure, shall as soon as practicable, report the same with the relative facts to the Secretary of the Navy.
(Signed) David G. Burnet
April 3, 1836[100]

An honest effort was made to give the above proclamation an immediate and wide publicity as shown in the files of Bailey Hardeman, Acting Secretary of State, and from a letter of John Forbes:

I had the honor of receiving today, your communication dated 3rd of April, 1836, in which, was enclosed a Proclamation for the suppression of the introduction of Africans or negroes into the Republic, excepting from the United States of America.
In compliance with your request, I shall have the

proclamation immediately carried to Nacogdoches, and have it published there or at Natchitoches as instructed.[101]

Laws Passed By Congress Under The Republic Regulating Slavery
An Act
Punishing Crimes and Misdemeanors

Section 6: ...Every person who shall steal or entice away any slave, out of or from the possession of the owner or owners of such slave, shall be deemed guilty of felony, and on conviction thereof, shall suffer death.[102]

An Act
Supplementary To An Act For The Punishment Of Crimes and Misdemeanors

Section 1: ...Be it enacted by the Senate and the House of Representatives of the Republic of Texas, in Congress Assembled, That if any person or persons shall introduce any African negro or negroes, contrary to the true intent and meaning of the Ninth Section of the general provisions of the Constitution, declaring the introduction of African negroes into this Republic to be piracy, except such as are from the United States of America, and had been held as slaves therein, to be guilty of piracy; and upon conviction thereof, before any court having cognizance of the same shall suffer death, without benefit of clergy.

Section 2: ...Be it further enacted, That if any person or persons shall introduce into the Republic of Texas, any Africans or any slave or slaves, from the United

States of America, except such slave or slaves as were previously introduced and held in slavery in that republic, in conformity with the laws of that government, shall be deemed guilty of piracy, and upon conviction thereof, before any court-having cognizance of the same, shall suffer death.[103]

Joint Resolution
For The Relief of Free Persons of Color

Resolved, by the Senate and House of Representatives of the Republic of Texas, in Congress assembled, That all free Africans or descendants of Africans, who were residing within the Republic of Texas at the date of the Declaration of Independence, and their natural issue, are hereby granted and allowed the privilege of remaining in any part of the Republic as long as they choose; on the condition of performing all duties required of them by law.

(Signed) B. T. Archer, Speaker of the House of Representatives
Jesse Grimes, President Pro tem. of the Senate
Sam Houston, President[104]
Approved, June 5, 1837

Section 9: ...Be it further enacted, That it shall not be lawful for any person of European blood or their descendants, to intermarry with Africans, or the descendants of Africans; and should any person as aforesaid violate the provisions of this section, such marriage shall be null and void, and the parties on conviction shall be deemed guilty of a high misdemeanor.[105]

An Act.
To Provide For the Punishment of Crimes and Misdemeanors Committed by Slaves and Free Persons of Color

Section 1: ...Be it enacted by the Senate and House of Representatives of the Republic of Texas, in Congress assembled, That from and after the passage of this act, the following shall be considered capital offenses when committed by a slave or free person of color, to wit: Insurrection or any attempt to excite it, poisoning or attempting to poison, committing rape or attempting it on any free white female, assaulting a free white person, with intent to kill, or with a weapon likely to produce death, or maiming a free white person, arson, murder, burglary, every and each of which offenses shall be triable in the district courts, and upon conviction shall he punished with death.

Section 2: ...Be it further enacted, That it shall not he lawful for any free person of color, to inveigle or entice away from their owner or master, any slave or slaves, not to aid or assist any slave or slaves to leave this Republic, without the consent of the owner of such slave or slaves; nor shall it he lawful for any free person of color to conceal or render aid or assistance to any runaway slave, with the intent to prevent the return of such runaway to his or her owner, and upon conviction of any of the foregoing offenses before the district courts such free person of color shall be fined in the sum equal to the value of such slave or slaves, and on failure to pay the said fine, shall he sold as a slave for life.

Section 3: ...Be it further enacted, That all other

crimes and misdemeanors, known to the Common Law of England, committed by slaves, shall he triable before the County Courts, and on conviction, shall be punishable at the discretion of said court, so as not to extend to life or limb.

Section 4: ...Be it further enacted, That upon complaint made upon oath to any member of the county court, of any offense not capital having been committed by any slave, it shall be the duty of said court forthwith to call a special term of said court for the trial of such slave, and when such special term may be called, it shall be the duty of the county court in conjunction with the sheriff to draw fifteen jurors, in the usual way to attend such term, and if any of them shall fail to attend, or from challenges the number of twelve should not be had, it shall be made up from the bystanders.

Section 5: ...Be it further enacted, That it shall not he necessary in such cases, that a bill he found by a grand jury, but the party shall he required to proceed to trial upon a charge made out and signed hy the person lodging the information setting forth the offense with which such slave stands charged.

Section 6: Be it further enacted, That if any slave or free person of color shall use insulting or abusive language to or threaten any free white person, upon complaint thereof before any justice of the peace, such justice shall cause such negro to he arrested, and upon conviction, the slave or free person of color, shall he punished by stripes not exceeding one hundred nor less than twenty-five.[106]

An Act
To Provide for the Foreclosing of Mortgages on Real and Personal Estates

Section 2: ...And be it further enacted, That all mortgages on negroes and other personal property shall be foreclosed in the following manner:

Any person or persons holding a mortgage on personal property, and wishing to foreclose the same, shall make application to the chief justice of the county, and make affidavit before him of the amount of principal and interest due thereon, which affidavit shall he annexed to such mortgage, and thereupon, the clerk of the county court shall issue execution as in cases of judgment, which execution being delivered to the sheriff shall be levied upon the mortgaged property, and after being advertised for at least sixty days in some public Gazette, shall be set up and sold to the highest bidder; provided always, that if any disputes shall arise as to the amount due on such mortgage, the chief justice of the county court shall order the sale to be postponed upon the defendant's entering into bond and security in double the amount of the mortgage, for the delivery to the sheriff of the property so levied upon; and the same shall be returned to, and triable at the next term of the court, as in other cases.[107]

An Act
To Punish Certain Offenses Therein Named

Section 1: ...Be it further enacted by the Senate and the House of Representatives of the Republic of Texas, in Congress assembled, That from after the passage of this act, if any person shall be found guilty of harboring or clandestinely supporting any runaway negro slave or negroes indentured for a term of years, or in aiding or assisting in so doing, on conviction thereof before a court of competent jurisdiction, he shall for such offense be fined in a sum of not less than five hundred nor more than one thousand dollars, shall be imprisoned not less than six months nor more than one year.[108]

An Act
Concerning Free Persons of Color

Section 1: ...Be it enacted by the Senate and House of Representatives of the Republic of Texas, in Congress assembled, That from and after the passage of this act, it shall not be lawful for any free person of color to emigrate to this Republic.

Section 2: ...Be it further enacted, That if any free person of color shall emigrate to this Republic, it shall be the duty of the sheriff, or any one of the constables of the county to which such emigration shall be made, to arrest such free persons of color, after giving them ten days' notice, and bring them before the Chief Justice of the county, or Judge of the district, before whom such free person of color may be brought, to receive the bond of such free person of color in the sum of one thousand dollars, with the security of a citizen, to be approved by him, conditioned for the removal of such free person of color out of the limits of the Republic.

Section 3: ...Be it further enacted, That if any free person of color should be brought before any Chief Justice of any County, or District Judge, and shall not be able to give the bond as prescribed in the second section of this act, such Chief Justice, or District Judge, shall commit, such free person of color to the public jail, with an order to the sheriff to expose him to the public to the highest bidder, at the court house door of his county, after giving four weeks' notice of the same, in the nearest public journal, and at least four public places in his county; and the said purchaser shall and may exercise all the rights of ownership over said free person of color, for one year from such sale.

Section 4: ...Be it further enacted, and if any such free person of color shall, during the year of such slavery, be able to give his bond as contemplated in the second section of this act, to take effect at the end of his slavery, he shall be permitted to do; but if he shall fail to render the bond, until after the expiration of his slavery, it shall be the duty of the purchaser to return him into the hands of the sheriff.

Section 5: ...Be it further enacted, It shall be the duty of the sheriff, upon the return of such free person of color, upon giving six weeks' notice in some public journal, and at least four public places in his county, to expose the free person of color so returned, at public sale, to the highest bidder; and such free person of color so sold shall remain a slave for life: Provided, That if any person of color so sold should be the property of any individual, he shall have his right of recovery by due course of law.

Section 6: ...Be it further enacted, All monies arising from the sale of such free person of color, shall be paid into the county treasury, subject to appropriation by the District Court for public purposes.

Section 7: ...Be it further enacted, upon the forfeiture of the bond of any free person of color, the same shall be placed in the hands of the District Attorney for collection, who shall prosecute the same against the securities only; and the amount of sale, if such shall have been made, for the free person of color, shall, in all cases, be subtracted from the amount adjudged against the securities, and the remainder only shall be recovered from them.

Section 8: ...Be it further enacted, That two years shall be allowed, from and after the passage of this act, to all free persons of color who are now in this Republic, to remove out of the same; and all those who shall be found here after that time, without the permission of Congress, shall be arrested and sold as provided in this act.

Section 9: ...Be it further enacted, That it shall not be lawful for any master of a vessel, or owner thereof, nor for any other person or persons whatsoever, to bring, import, induce, or aid or assist in the bringing, importing, or inducing any free person of color within the limits of Texas, directly or indirectly; and any person so offending shall be deemed guilty of a misdemeanor, and on conviction shall be fined in the sum of not less than one nore more than ten thousand dollars: Provided, That cooks and other hands employed on board of vessels shall not be considered as coming within the provisions of this act.

Section 10: ...Be it further enacted, That the President of the Republic do issue his proclamation, commanding all free persons of color who are now in the Republic, to remove from the same before the first of

January, 1842, and the Secretary of State publish this act a number of times in all the journals of this Republic.[109]

An Act
Concerning Slaves

Section 1: ...Be it further enacted by the Senate and the House of Representatives of the Republic of Texas, in Congress assembled, That if any person shall hereafter sell to any slave, without the written consent of his or her master, mistress or overseer, the ardent spirits or intoxicating liquors, he or she so offending shall forfeit and pay on conviction thereof, any sum not less than twenty dollars nor more than two hundred dollars.

Section 2: ...Be it further enacted, That if any person shall buy from any slave, any cotton, com, meat or other valuable produce or article whatever, without the written consent of his or her master, or mistress, or overseer, he or she is offending, shall on conviction thereof be fined in any sum not less than twenty nor more than two hundred dollars, with the value to the owner of any property sold.

Section 3: ...Be it further enacted, That if any person shall unreasonably or cruelly treat, or otherwise abuse any slave, he or she shall be liable to be sued in any court of competent jurisdiction, and on conviction thereof, shall be fined in a sura, not less than two hundred and fifty dollars, nor more than two thousand dollars.

Section 4: ...Be it further enacted, That if any person

or persons shall murder any slave, or so cruelly treat the same as to cause death, the same shall be felony, and punished as in other cases of murder.

Section 5: ...Be it further enacted, That it shall be the duty of the District Judges within said Republic, to carry into effect the foregoing provisions of this act.

Section 6: ...Be it further enacted, That no slave in this Republic shall carry a gun or other deadly weapon without the written consent of his master, mistress or overseer; such arms or weapons shall he liable to be taken by any person from any such negro, and all such property forfeited, if it does not exceed ten dollars in value; but any such property may be reclaimed by the owner on paying ten dollars to the person who may have taken the same.[110]

An Act
Concerning Certain Free Persons of Color

Section 1: ...Be it enacted by the Senate and the House of Representatives of the Republic of Texas in Congress assembled, That Samuel McCulloch Jr. and his three sisters to wit: Jane, Harriett, and Mahalay, and their descendants, better known as the free children of Sam McCulloch Sr., now in the Republic of Texas, together with a free colored girl, known by the name of Ulde or Hulder, a member of said McCulloch's family, be, and in the same are here from henceforth, exempted from the provisions of "An Act Concerning Free Persons of Color," approved the fifth of February, 1840.

Section 2: ...Be it further enacted, That the afore said

free persons, be, and hereby from henceforth are permitted and allowed to continue their residence within the bounds of the Republic of Texas.

An Act
Prohibiting Forced Sale of Slaves Under Execution

Section 1: ...Be it enacted by the Senate and the House of Representatives of the Republic of Texas, in Congress assembled, That hereafter no slave or slaves or indentured free person or persons, in the possession and ownership of the bona fide master, or heir or heirs, legatee or legatees of any intestate or deceased person, shall be subject to forced sales, by virtue of any writ of venditioni exponas, fieri facias, or execution of any kind; Provided, always, That the provisions of this act shall not be construed to extend to sales under or by virtue of any final decree or judgment of the courts of competent jurisdiction, where the same has been made or obtained in conformity to law, ordering the sale and distribution of the property of any intestate or deceased persons' estate upon petition, as directed, being filed, praying for the same; Provided, nothing herein shall protect said property in the possession or ownership of defaulters to this Republic.[111]

An Act
Regulating the Sale of Runaway Slaves

Section 1: ...Be it enacted by the Senate and the House of Representatives of the Republic of Texas, in Congress assembled, That where any slave is now in the jail of any county of the Republic, or shall hereafter be committed to the jail thereof as a runaway, a notice of the apprehension and commitment, with a full description of the said slave, shall be published weekly in one of the Gazettes at the seat of Government, for the space of one month, and printed copies thereof shall be furnished to the Clerk of the County Court of the county in which the commitment is made, to be carefully filed and preserved in his office, and it shall be the duty of the sheriff or jailor having custody of said slave, as ascertain as nearly as may be, the name of the owner thereof, and to address him or her by regular post, at least twice, giving a full description of said runaway, in such manner as may best lead to the discovery and restoration.

Section 2: ...Be it further enacted, That if said runaway slave shall not be claimed and proved by the owner thereof within six months of the first publication of the commitment of said slave, as aforesaid, the Sheriff of the County in which the commitment was made, shall expose said slave to sale at public outcry at the court house of his proper county, upon giving at least thirty days' previous notice of such sale, by advertising posted up in at least two public places in said county having a gazette, and out of the proceeds arising from the sale of any runaway slave as aforesaid, the sheriff shall be entitled to the same commission and fees as are allowed in cases of execution, and the balance after paying all prison fees, or fees for the maintenance of said runaway while in custody. Clerk's fees, and expenses of advertising and apprehending, shall be paid into the county treasury for the use of the proper county; provided, that if the owner of any runaway slave thus sold, should prove his property in said slave within three years after said sale, the proper county shall pay to him the amount that shall have been paid into the county treasury, on account of the sale of said slave, but the right to any slave sold as aforesaid, shall be and remain vested in the purchaser under the sale made by the sheriff as aforesaid, any law to the contrary notwithstanding.

Section 3: ...Be it further enacted, That the sheriff making the sale of any runaway as aforesaid, shall then return a full and clear account and statement of such sale under his hand and seal, to the clerk of the county court, who shall record the same among the records of deeds.

Section 4: ...Be it further enacted, That all runaway slaves shall be lawfully apprehended by any person, and carried before the next Justice of the Peace, who shall commit them to the county jail, or the custody of the sheriff, or send them to the owner, if known, who shall pay for every slave so taken up, the sura of ten dollars to the person apprehending him or her, and all reasonable costs and damages; and if said owner shall fail or refuse to pay said reward and reasonable expenses, the person apprehending and delivering said runaway slaves as aforesaid, shall be entitled to have his action for the recovery of the same before any Justice of the Peace of the district or precinct in which said owner resides, or in which said slave is delivered up to the owner as aforesaid.

Section 5: ...Be it further enacted, That if any person or persons being convicted, harboring or concealing any negro or negroes belonging to any person or persons whatsoever, or suffering the same so to be, with his consent or knowledge, shall upon conviction of such offense, be fined in the sum exceeding five hundred dollars, and shall be imprisoned not less than one calendar month, nor exceeding six calendar months, and shall be liable in damages to the party injured, to be recovered by action on the case, before any court having competent jurisdiction.

Section 6: ...Be it further enacted, That this act be in force and take effect from and after its passage.

An Act
To Repeal an Act Entitled:
"An Act Prohibiting Forced Sale of Slaves"

Be it enacted by the Senate and House of Representatives of the Republic of Texas, in Congress assembled, That "An act prohibiting forced sale of slaves under execution" approved. January 27, 1841, and the same is hereby repealed.
Approved 30th December, 1841.

An Act
To Amend an Act Entitled:
"An Act to Raise a Revenue by Direct Taxation"
Approved January 16, 1840

Section 1: ...Be it enacted by the Senate and the House of Representatives of the Republic of Texas, in Congress assembled, That from and after the first day of April, 1842, the following shall be the rate of taxes on all property, capital, and other objects, hereinafter specified, together with the tax on licences to pursue any vocation or calling herein mentioned: On all slaves under ten years of age, twenty-five cents each; and on all between ten years and sixty years, the sum of seventy-five cents.[112]

**An Act
Supplementary to "An Act Regulating The Sale of
Runaway Slaves" Approved January 5, 1841.**

Section 1: ...Be it enacted by the Senate and the House of Representatives of the Republic of Texas, in Congress assembled, That it shall be lawful, hereafter, for any person, or persons, who may apprehend and commit to jail any runaway slave, or slaves, on or west of the San Antonio River, to demand and receive the sum of fifty dollars for each and every slave, so apprehended, provided, said slave or slaves so secured, that the property come safely to the possession of the owner, to be paid upon the delivery of such slave, or slaves, to the owner thereof, or his authorized agent; and the person, or persons, apprehending such slaves, shall have a lien on the same, until the reward specified, as aforesaid, be paid.

Section 2: ...Be it further enacted, That in all cases where a slave or slaves shall be apprehended and delivered to the owner at his residence, it shall be lawful for the person apprehending and delivering such slave or slaves, to demand and receive, for each slave so apprehended and delivered, in addition to the sura specified, as aforesaid, the further sum of two dollars for every thirty miles he may travel in going and returning from the residence of said owner, the distance to be computed over the shortest route traveled at the time, and to have a lien upon the slave or slaves, for the payment of the same, as provided for in the first section of this act.

Section 3: ...Be it further enacted, That the provisions of the second section of this act shall extend to persons apprehending runaway slaves in any part of the Republic, provided, said slaves are delivered by the apprehender to the owner thereof, at his or her residence.

Section 4: ...Be it further enacted, That if no owner appears and claims any slave or slaves so apprehended, and the same be sold under the provisions of the act to which this ia a supplement, then and in that case, it shall be the duty of the sheriff to pay over to the person, or persons, apprehending such slave, or slaves, the reward prescribed by the provisions of the first section of this act; provided, that the sheriff shall take, in writing, the testimony on which the claim to the reward is admitted, and that the same be filed in the office of the Clerk of the County Court.

Section 5: ...Be it further enacted, That this act take effect and be in force from and after its passage.[113]

Laws of the State of Texas Prior to Secession
Regulating Negro Slavery
Constitutional Provisions
Bill of Rights.

Section 2: ...All freemen, when they form a social compact, have equal rights; and no man, or set of men, is entitled to exclusive, separate, public emoluments or privileges, but in consideration of public services.

Article Third
Legislative Department[114]

Section 1: ...Every free male person who shall have attained the age of twenty-one years, and who shall be a citizen of the United States, or who is at the time of the adoption of this Constitution by the Congress of the United States, a citizen of the Republic of Texas, and shall have resided in this State one year next preceding an election, and the last six months within the district, county, city or town in which he offers to vote, (Indians not taxed, Africans and descendants of Africans excepted) shall be deemed a qualified elector.

Section 2: ...All free male persons over the age of twenty-one years, (Indians not taxed. Africans and descendants of Africans excepted) who shall have resided six months in Texas, immediately preceding the acceptance of this Constitution by the Congress of the United States, shall be deemed qualified electors.

Article Eighth
Slaves

Section 1: ...The Legislature shall have no power to pass laws for the emancipation of slaves, without the consent of their owners; nor without paying their owners, previous to such emancipation, a full equivalent in money, for the slaves so emancipated. They shall have no power to prevent emigrants to this State, from bringing with them such persons as are deemed slaves by the laws of any of the United States, so long as any person of the same age or description shall be continued in slavery, by the laws of this State; provided, that such slave be the bona fide property of such emigrants; Provided, also, that the laws shall be passed to inhibit the introduction, into this State, of slaves who have committed high crimes in other States or territories. They shall have the right to pass laws to permit the owners of Slaves to emancipate them, saving the rights of creditors, and preventing them from becoming a public charge. They shall have full power to pass laws, which will oblige the owners of slaves to treat them with humanity; to provide for them, necessary food and clothing; to abstain from all injuries to them, extending to life or limb; and in case of their neglect or refusal to comply with the directions of such laws, to have such slave or slaves taken from such owner, and sold for the benefit of such owner or owners. They may pass laws to prevent slaves from being brought into this State as merchandise only.

Section 2: ...In the prosecution of slaves for crimes of a higher grade than petit larceny, the Legislature shall have no power to deprive them of an impartial trial by petit jury.

Section 3: ...Any person who shall maliciously dismember or deprive a slave of life, shall suffer such punishment as would be inflicted, in case of the life offense had been committed upon a free white person, and on the like proof, except in case of insurrection of such slave.

Statutes of the State of Texas
Prior to Secession

To Prevent Slaves From Hiring Their Own Time, or Their Owners From Hiring Them to Other Slaves. Free Negroes, or Mulattoes

Section 1: ...That the owner of the slave shall be fined in a sum not to exceed one hundred dollars for each offense.

Section 2: ...That all slaves going at large shall be taken up and taken before a Justice of the Peace.

Section 3: ...That if the Justice of the Peace receives satisfactory evidence of slaves at large within his county, he shall issue warrant and bring such offenders before him.

Section 4: ...That such slaves shall be committed to the county jail.

Section 5: ...That upon payment of costs and fine that may have accrued by master, said slave may be discharged.

Section 6: ...That the Justice of the Peace may report the committing of any slave under this act to the next session of the County Court.

Section 7: ...That the County Court shall give notice of slaves committed since the last session of the same and order the clerk of the County- Court to publish same.

Section 8: ...That the slave advertised according to Section 7 if not proven by any owner, the court shall order sale on a certain day not less than three months nor more than six months, and that publication be made in some newspaper published in the State, at least for three months next before the said day of sale, and the sheriff shall sell the said slave for cash, under the same regulations that govern sales under execution, unless the said slave be proven away by the owner, under provisions of Section 5 of this act.

Section 9: ...That all fines arising under this act shall be paid to the County Treasury, after paying the costs of apprehending, trying, committing, advertising, and five per cent to the sheriff for selling, and all other costs necessarily accruing. All such monies are to be subject to the orders of the County Court for county purposes.

Section 10: ...That if any person, within five years after the sale of a slave under this act, shall come forward and make satisfactory proof to the county court, that said slave was his property at the time of such sale, the court shall order the county to pay out of any money in the treasury not otherwise appropriated, to said person, the balance of such sale after deducting all costs and fine that had accrued against the same.[115]

An Act to Amend an Act

That the third section of an Act, entitled an "Act Concerning Slaves," approved February 5th, 1840, be so amended as to read as follows, to wit: That if any person or persons shall cruelly or unreasonably treat or abuse any slave belonging to him, her, or them, or to another or others, he, she, or they and each of them shall be liable to indictment or presentment, as for Misdemeanor, in the District Court, and on conviction thereof, may be fined for each and every such offense, not less than twenty dollars, nor more than five hundred dollars.[116]

An Act
Authorizing and Requiring the County Courts To Regulate Roads and Appoint Overseers

Section 7: It shall be the duty of the overseers of any road to give two days previous notice by summons in person or in writing, left at their respective places of abode, to all free male persons, as well as to the owners, overseers, or employers of slaves liable to work on the roads in his precinct, to meet at such time and place as he shall designate, and bring with them such tools to work with on the roads as he shall direct; all slaves refusing to appear may be fined in the sum of one dollar for each and every day he fails to attend, the fine to be collected from his owner, overseer, or employer.

Section 13: Any slave, his master, or overseer may by calling on the road overseer any time before the day appointed to work on roads and paying the amount for which he or they might be liable for failure to appear, be exempt from such work or from penalty.

Section 15: All male slaves between the ages of fifteen and fifty shall be among those liable to work on the roads.

Joint Resolution on the "Provision" Slavery,

The Tariff, and the War Against Mexico

Section 1: Resolved, That any attempt on the part of the Congress of the United States to interfere with the domestic and internal policies of the States or territories, is unwarranted by the Constitution of the United States, and in violation of the rights of the States. The "Proviso" if submitted to, would prevent the slave-holding States from enjoying the full benefits of any territory which may be hereafter acquired by the United States. The Constitution of the United States recognizes slavery, as one of our domestic institutions, and we acknowledge no right to abolish it, but that which belongs to the slave-holding States themselves. We will not submit to any law, which prohibits the citizens of the Southern States from taking their property to any territory which may be acquired from Mexico. We are willing to submit to the compromises of the Constitution, but we will never submit to a usurpation of power which robs us of our rights.[117]

An Act To Amend An Act

That the sixth section of an act entitled "An Act Concerning Slaves" approved 5th February, 1840, be amended so as to read as follows:

That any slave who may be found away from the premises of his owner, overseer, or employer, on Sunday, or after the hour of ten o'clock P.M. of any other day, without a written permit, or away from the route usually travelled in going to and returning from the place to which the permit extends, the said slave shall be liable to be taken up by any patrol, justice of the peace, or individual; in case taken up by the patrol, the said patrol shall inflict as punishment not more than ten lashes; if the patrol deemed that more than ten lashes were needed, he should take the slave to a justice of the peace, who upon notice from the master, shall adjudge the number of stripes which shall be inflicted, not exceeding nine; should the master be unknown, or should he reside at a greater distance from the place where the justice of the peace resides than it is to the nearest county jail, the said justice shall commit the slave to the said county jail, and cause notice to be given in writing to the master, the master to be entitled to said slave upon the payment of all reasonable costs and charges not exceeding ten dollars.

That it shall not be permissible for any slave to own firearms, and that any owner, overseer, or employer who shall knowingly permit any slave owned by him to carry firearms at other places than the premises of said owner, overseer, or employer shall be fined not less than twenty-five dollars nor more than one hundred dollars, and all costs, the firearms to be forfeited to the use of the county, and the negro receive not less than thirty-nine nor more than fifty lashes.

That any slave found with any articles of trade in his possession offering the same for sale without a written permit to sell, shall be adjudged by any justice of the peace before whom he may receive not more than thirty-nine lashes, and the articles of trade forfeited and sold to pay the costs, excess to be paid into the county treasury.

That any slave attempting to take the life of any white person or slave by poison or otherwise shall be delivered to the civil authorities by the owner, overseer, or employer; in case of refusal to deliver slave or to assist or connive at the escape of such slave, the owner, overseer, or employer shall be fined not less than one hundred nor more than five hundred dollars in addition to penalties imposed on accessories before or after the fact: Provided, that nothing herein contained shall be so construed as to interfere with or in anywise affect the right of incorporated towns and cities in this State in making and enforcing their own police regulations, except as far as it relates to the carrying of firearms.[118]

An Act.
To Enable Part Owners of Slaves To Obtain Partition Thereof

Section 1: That part owners of slaves and other personal property may be compelled to make partition between them.

Section 2: That the separate value of the slaves to which each party claiming partition may be entitled, shall be ascertained by the verdict of the jury.

Section 3: Where partition of slaves is ordered, execution shall be issued to the proper county officer where the property may be, commanding him to put the parties in possession of the property allotted to each respectively.

Section 4: When slaves will not admit of partition in kind, the jury shall so find by their verdict and ascertain the proportion of the value of such slaves.

Section 5: Officers of the county in which the property is situated, in cases covered by section four, may be empowered to sell the property and pay over the proceeds of the sale to the parties according to the judgment of the court.

Section 6: This act shall not affect partition of estates of deceased persons among the heirs and legatees.[119]

An Act
To Indemnify the Owners for the Loss of Slaves Executed For Capital Offenses

When a slave, the property of a citizen of the State shall be convicted of a capital offense, the jury rendering the verdict, shall assess the value of such slave; in case the punishment to the slave is death, the master shall receive from the State Treasury one-half of the appraised value, the appraisement not to exceed one thousand dollars, provided the owner shall not attempt to evade or defeat the execution of the law on said slave, nor shall a slave so paid for, who may be condemned for any offense, in the commission of which his owner was either principal or accessory.[120]

An Act
Concerning Offenses Committed by Negroes

Section 1: That if a free negro plot murder or by any means cause bodily injury to a white person with intent to kill, he shall be punished at the discretion of the jury, either with death, or by confinement in the penitentiary, not less than three nor more than ten years.

Section 2: That if a free negro attempt to marry a

white female or take from any person having lawful charge of her a white female child under twelve years of age, he shall he punished by death.

Section 3: That if a free negro commit any other offense not specified in this act, he shall be punished as a free white person.

Section 4: That if a slave plot or conspire to rebel or make insurrection, or commit offense for the commission of which a free negro is punishable with death, or by confinement in the penitentiary for not less than three years, he shall be punished with death.

Section 5: That if a slave commit an offense for which a free negro might be punished by confinement in the penitentiary for a period less than three years, such slave shall be punished by stripes, not exceeding fifty, at the discretion of the jury.

Section 6: That if a slave commit an offense, the commission of which, by a free person, is punishable as a misdemeanor, he shall be punished by stripes not exceeding thirty-nine.

Section 7: That a negro shall be punished with not exceeding thirty-nine stripes for the commission of the following offenses: (1) for using provoking language or menacing gestures to a white person; (2) for punishing a slave without the consent of his master, any pass, permit or token of his being from home without authority; (3) if he keep or carry firearms, sword or other weapon, or balls, or ammunition, besides forfeiting such articles in his possession; (4) if guilty of being in a riot, or making seditious speeches;

(5) if he sell or attempt to sell, or prepare, or administer any medicine, except by his master's order, in his family, or in the family of another, with the consent of such other, and except also, when a free negro administers medicine in his own family, or in the family of another person with the consent of such other.

Section 8: That the word negro, in this or any other statute of this State, shall also be construed to mean mulatto and every person who has one-fourth part or more of negro blood shall be deemed a mulatto.

Section 9: That the punishment of a negro by stripes shall be at the discretion of the jury as not to affect life, and when assessed by a justice shall not exceed fifty lashes.

Section 10: That the trial of negroes charged with felonious homicide, or any offense punishable with death, shall be in the District Courts, where the proceedings shall be as in the case of white persons.

Section 11: That on any indictment of a negro in the District Court, the accused may be found guilty of the offense charged, but guilty of any offense of which a free white person might be found guilty on such indictment, and the jury may find and assess such punishment against him as the offense would justify, if the negro had been charged therewith in the county court as in hereinafter provided.

Section 12: That the county courts of each county, to consist of the Chief-Justice, and two commissioners at least, or of three commissioners at least, in case of disability or of absence of the Chief-Justice, or vacancy in that office, shall be a criminal tribunal for the trial of negroes and slaves charged with felony, except in the cases provided for in the two preceding sections.

Section 13: That such, trials shall be on sworn information, or charge in writing entered of record, but without a grand jury, or a presentment or indictment.

Section 14: That free negroes charged with any offense in the county courts, and slaves charged with offenses punishable by death, shall be entitled to trial by jury of twelve good and lawful men, freeholders of the county, and shall have the same right of challenge allowed by law to white persons.

Section 15: That no one interested in a slave charged with crime shall sit on his trial as a member of the court or as a juror.

Section 16: That in criminal cases before the county court, if no counsel be employed by private persons, the court may employ some competent attorney who shall be entitled to compensation agreed upon to be paid out of the county treasury.

Section 17: That on trial of slaves for felony, the court shall assign counsel to defend, if none be employed, and allow fee not to exceed one hundred dollars, which shall be paid by the owner of the slave.

Section 18: That a regular term of the County Court for trial of negroes may be had on the first Monday of every month.

Section 19: That the clerk of the county court shall be

the clerk of the tribunal established by this act., and shall be entitled to receive the same fees and compensation that the clerk of the district court would be entitled to receive for similar services.

Section 20: That trial, upon showing of good cause, may be continued from term to term, not exceeding two continuances.

Section 21: That on a charge against a negro for felony, the court or jury may find the accused not guilty of the offense charged, but guilty of any offense for which a free white person might be found guilty on an indictment for such felony, and may assess the punishment therefor where it is not fixed by law, and give judgment accordingly.

Section 22: That if a slave or negro condemned to death escape and be retaken, the jailor or sheriff shall promptly inform the said court of the fact, and the court shall cause the sentence to be carried into effect on a day appointed by it.

Section 23: That a slave shall be tried for a misdemeanor by a justice of the county in which the offense is committed.

Section 24: That a free negro shall be tried for a misdemeanor by such justice punishable by stripes. For any other misdemeanor, he or she may be tried in the county court, but a justice of the peace before whom a free negro is charged with misdemeanor punishable by fine and imprisonment, or either, may try him or her and inflict such punishment as he would inflict on a slave for the same offense, or commit or recognize him for trial at the next court of the county.

Section 25: That in the case of a negro convicted of a misdemeanor by a justice, the decision may be removed by certiorari to the county court by the negro if free, or if he be a slave, by his owner; such negro shall, unless let to bail, be committed by the justice fo jail, until the next term of such court, and the witnesses shall also be recognized to appear at the same time.

Section 26: That every such certiorari shall be tried in the county court without pleadings in writing and without continuance, except for good cause shown.

Section 27: That the chief justices of the several counties shall have power to issue writs of certiorari in any case arising under this act.[121]

An Act
Making Appropriation for the Indemnification of the Owners of Slaves Executed for Crimes

That the sum of five thousand dollars is hereby appropriated for the indemnification of the owners of slaves executed since the 24th of January, A.D. 1852. That this appropriation be made purpose of carrying out the provisions of an act entitled to indemnify the owners for the loss of slaves executed for capital offenses, approved January 24, 1852.[122]

An Act
Supplemental to An Act Concerning Crimes and Punishments.

Approved March 20, 1848

Section 4: Every person who shall unlawfully sell any free person for a slave, or hold any free person as a slave against his will, knowing the person so sold or held to be free, shall be punished by confinement to hard labor in the penitentiary not less than one year nor more than ten years, or by fine not exceeding one thousand dollars, and imprisonment in the county jail not exceeding one year.

Section 6: Murder or manslaughter committed upon the body of a slave shall be punished in the same manner as murder or manslaughter committed upon the body of a free white person.[123]

An Act
Supplemental to An Act Concerning Crimes and Punishments.

Approved March 20. 1848

Offenses Against Slaves and Slave Property

Section 46: If any person advise or conspire with a slave to rebel or make insurrection, or with any person to induce a slave to rebel or make insurrection, he shall be punished with death, whether such rebellion or insurrection be made or not.

Section 47: The master of any steamboat or other vessel who shall carry or cause to be carried out of any county a slave, without the consent of the owner or employer, with intent to deprive the owner of such slave, or who shall knowingly receive on board any runaway slave, and permit him to remain on board without proper efforts to apprehend him, shall be confined in the penitentiary not less than two nor more than ten years.

Section 48: Every person who shall steal, take and carry away, or entice away any slave, the property of another, shall be punished by confinement to hard labor in the penitentiary not less than three nor exceeding fifteen years.

Section 49: Every person who shall attempt to steal or entice away a slave from the owner or employer, shall be confined in the penitentiary not less than one nor more than ten years.

Section 50: If a free person advise any slave to abscond from his master or employer, or aid such slave to abscond, by procuring or delivering to him a pass or other writing, or by furnishing him money, clothes, provisions or other facility, he shall be confined in the penitentiary not less than three nor more than five years.

Section 51: If any master of a vessel or other person shall knowingly import or he caught bringing any slave who shall be a fugitive from justice, or shall have been sold or convicted for crime beyond the limits of this State, he shall be confined in jail not less than six months, and fined one hundred dollars.[124]

Joint Resolution

Resolved, That this State regards the act of Congress passed in 1850 admitting California into the Union, fixing the boundary of Texas etc., as a question fully settled so far as related to the question of slavery and that Texas is opposed to any change in those laws affecting their principles on the great questions which have so unhappily divided the Northern and Southern States of the Union.

That the State of Texas regards the fugitive slave law of 1850 as a measure of constitutional right and justice to the slave-holding States, and will look upon the repeal of this law or its modification as an invasion of her constitutional rights.

That the State of Texas regards the late act known as the Kansas-Nebraska Act as a measure founded in the true spirit of the Federal Constitution, and will look upon the repeal or modification of this law as an invasion of her constitutional rights.

An Act
To Prevent Slaves from Carrying Guns or Other Dangerous Weapons

Section 1: That no slave shall carry a gun on the premises of owner without the written permit of the owner.

Section 2: That no slave shall carry a gun or other deadly weapon beyond the premises of owner or employer unless accompanied by owner or some white person authorized by the owner.

Section 3: That any gun or weapon found on a slave contrary to above provisions may be forfeited to person finding such slave with the weapon, provided the weapon is valued at not more than twenty dollars. Any such property may be reclaimed by the owner upon payment of twenty dollars.[125]

An Act
To Amend the Ninth Section of An Act Approved February 5, 1840. Concerning Free Persons of Color

That it shall not be lawful for any master of a vessel or owner thereof, nor any other person to bring, induce or aid or assist any free person of color within the limits of the State of Texas, directly or indirectly. Any person so offending is subject to a fine not less than hundred dollars nor more than two thousand dollars.[126]

An Act
To Permit Free Persons of African Descent To Select Their Own Masters and Become Slaves

Section 1: That it shall be lawful for any free person of African descent over fourteen years of age, now in this State, to choose his of her master, and become a slave; provided said slave shall not be subject to forced sales for any debt incurred or judgment rendered against the chosen master prior to the period of enslavement.

Section 2: That said person desiring to become a slave shall file a petition with the District Court of the county of which he or she resides.

Section 3: That the Court shall, upon appearance in open court of both, petitioner and person designated in the petition as desired master, proceed to examine each separately, as well as witnesses to said petition;

that if upon examination the court shall be satisfied that there is no fraud nor collusion, the petition shall be granted, and the condition of the petitioner shall in all respects be the same as though the petitioner had been born a slave to the master so chosen.

Section 4: That in case the petitioner be a female with children under fourteen years of age, and shall in her petition ask that such children become the slaves of the same person chosen by her as master, it shall also decree such children to be slaves of the same owner; provided that where the children's mother shall be deceased, the next friend of such children shall have authority to proceed in the same manner as the mother might do under this act.

Section 5: The District Attorney shall be entitled to a fee of ten dollars, for each examination, which shall be costs in the proceedings, and all such costs shall be paid by the master to whom the slave may be decreed.[127]

An Act
To Encourage the Reclamation of Slaves Escaping Beyond the Slave Territories of the United States

Section 1: That any person capturing or causing to be captured a slave or slaves escaping beyond the limits of the slave territories of the United States and delivering such slave or slaves to the Sheriff of Travis County shall be entitled to receive from the Treasury of the State thirty- three and one-third per cent of the value of such slave or slaves.

Section 2: That any person capturing a slave or

slaves, as provided above, shall after arriving within the limits of this State in the first organized county which he may reach, go before a Judge of the District Court, Chief Justice, Notary Public, or Clerk of the District or County Court, and make proof to the satisfaction of such officer, by at least two witnesses, that the slave or slaves so captured were taken beyond the limits of the slave territory of the United States, whereupon such officer shall certify to the fact of said proof, under his hand and seal, if he have one, and deliver the same to the party so appearing before him. Upon arriving at the City of Austin, in the County of Travis, the captor shall deliver such slave or slaves to the Sheriff of said county, who shall without delay summon two freeholders, citizens of said county, to appraise such slave or slaves under oath, and he shall append to the certificate of proof, said appraisement together with his certificate that they have been delivered to him and are in his custody, and upon presentation of the same to the Comptroller, that officer shall issue his warrant on the Treasurer, for the amount of thirty-three and one-third per cent of the appraisement, to be paid out of any money in the Treasury not otherwise appropriated.

Section 3: That it shall be the duty of said Sheriff to advertise such slave or slaves in the official paper of the State for three months, giving therein a full description of the same, appraised value, and name of the reputed owner; should the owner appear, he shall be entitled to receive the same upon payment of the one-third appraised valuation with interest thereon at the rate of eight per cent per annum and also five per cent of the appraised value of said slave shall remain in the Treasury as an accumulating fund to be applied to the purposes contemplated in this act, and all other legal charges.

Section 4: That should the owner fail to prove property and pay charges, it shall be the duty of the Sheriff to advertise such slave or slaves for sale, giving thirty days notice in some newspaper in the City of Austin, and at the expiration of such period shall sell the said slave or slaves at auction to the highest bidder for cash; and after paying all the necessary and legal charges shall pay the remainder over to the Treasurer who shall reimburse the State for the amount originally paid for their apprehension, and shall retain the remainder subject to the order of the owner or owners of such slaves.

Section 6: That any person capturing a slave as contemplated by the preceding sections of this act shall deliver the same to the owner to any portion of this State, shall be entitled to receive the same compensation as if delivered to the Sheriff of Travis County and shall be entitled to hold possession of such slave or slaves as security therefor until paid.[128]

The Penal Code of Texas

Article 796: An offense committed by a slave is known as a felony when the punishment therefor is death or branding. An offense committed by a free person of color, is known as a felony when the punishment for the same is death, branding, or imprisonment in the penitentiary; all other offenses committed by either of these classes of persons, are called petty offenses.

Article 797: The District Court alone has jurisdiction to try felonies committed by either slaves or free persons of color; the jurisdiction for the trial of petty offenses, belongs to the Courts of Justices of the Peace, Layors and Recorders.

Article 801: A slave or free person of color when tried for penal offense, is in law a person, but his personal rights are to be controlled by the provisions of this Part of the Penal Code, and are subject to rules different from those which would be applied in the case of a free white person, arising from the peculiar position of these classes of persons in society.

Article 802: But if the chastisement be unreasonable and excessive, the killing will be manslaughter.

Article 804: Patrols or others, authorized by law to punish slaves, may inflict moderate chastisement, and the rights and duties of a slave, under such circumstances, are governed by the same rules which would apply to the case of the master enforcing lawful obedience.

Article 806: A free person of color residing in the State in violation of law, is, in all respects, upon a footing of equality, as to his personal rights, with a slave.

Article 807: In every case of offenses committed by slaves against the person of free persons of color, or of free persons of color against the persons of slaves, the parties are deemed to stand upon terms of equality.

Article 808: If it shall appear on trial of any slave or

free person of color, for the killing of, or personal injury to a white person, that the person killed or injured was in the habit of association with slaves or free negroes, and by his general conduct placed himself upon an equality with these classes of persons, the rights of the slave or person of color are to be governed by the same rules which would apply if the offense had been committed upon the person of a slave or person of color, except in cases where the person injured is a minor, under the age of eighteen years.

Article 809: The preceding article does not apply where the injury was done to the master of the slave, or to any member of the family of the master of the slave.

Article 811: Slaves are not punishable by fine, or by imprisonment in the penitentiary or house of correction.

Article 812: There shall be four types of punishment for slaves: death, branding, standing in the pillory, and whipping.

Article 813: The punishment of death is inflicted by hanging, in the same manner as in the case of free white persons.

Article 814: The punishment of branding is inflicted with a hot iron, in the shape of the letter "C," upon the left cheek.

Article 815: The punishment of branding shall be so inflicted as to produce no greater pain than that which is unavoidable, and in such manner only as to leave an indelible impression, and not to lacerate the cheek.

Article 816: The punishment of whipping is inflicted upon the bare back, and when not specially directed otherwise, it shall in all cases he construed to mean thirty-nine lashes.

Article 818: If in any county a Public Pillory be erected by the County Court, punishment by standing in the Pillory may be substituted for all offenses punishable by whipping, or, in aggravated cases, the punishment of the Pillory may be added to that of whipping.

Article 820: The following offenses, when committed by slaves, shall be punished by branding: burglary, robbery; assaults with intent to commit murder, rape, or robbery; attempts to commit arson, or rape; assault with a deadly weapon upon a white person in any case except self-defense; theft, manslaughter.

Article 821: All offenses not specially enumerated, when committed by slaves, shall be punished by whipping, which may be public or private, at the discretion of the jury or court.

Article 822: Free persons of color are subject to the following punishments: death, branding, imprisonment in the penitentiary, whipping or standing in the pillory, and labor upon any public works of a county.

Article 824: Arson, robbery, aiding in an insurrection of slaves, rape of a free white female, when committed by a free person of color, shall be punished by death, or by imprisonment in the penitentiary, for life, or a term of years.

Article 825: For any of the offenses named in the two preceding Articles, if the defendant be sentenced to the penitentiary, branding may be also added as a part of the punishment.

Article 828: A free person of color found guilty of theft to the amount of twenty dollars or more, shall be punished by whipping, and shall, in addition thereto, be subject to be compelled to work upon the road or any public work of the county where he is convicted, under the direction of the County Court, for a term not exceeding six months.[129]

Title XVII — Chapter VI — Section IV
Justified Homicide of a Slave

Article 564: Homicide committed upon a slave is justifiable in the following cases:

1. When the slave is in a state of insurrection.

2. When a slave forcibly resists any lawful order of his master, overseer, or other person having legal charge of him, in such manner as to give reasonable fear of loss of life, or great bodily harm, in enforcing obedience to such order.

3. Where a runaway slave forcibly resists a person attempting to arrest him, in such manner as to cause reasonable fear of loss of life, or of great bodily harm, in making such arrest.

4. Where a slave forcibly resists any lawful order of

any patrol or officer of the law, in such manner as to cause reasonable fear of loss of life, or great bodily harm, in executing such order.

5. When a slave uses weapons calculated to produce death, or in any case other than those in which he may lawfully resist with arms, under the provisions of Part III of this Code.

Article 565: A slave is said to be in a state of insurrection when he is acting in concert with at least four others, and they are armed with the intention of freeing one or more of their number from a state of slavery.

Article 566: Flight on the part of a slave, except when in a state of insurrection, does not justify homicide by either the master or any other person; and the killing of a slave under any other circumstances except those above enumerated, is the same offense as the killing of a free white person.[130]

Title 12 — Chapter I
Unlawful Marriage

Article 386 shall hereafter read as follows: If any white person shall, within this state, knowingly marry a negro, or a person of mixed blood, descended from negro ancestry, to the third generation inclusive, though an ancestor of each generation may have been a white person, or having so married in or out of this state, shall continue within this state to cohabit with such negro, he or she shall be punished by confinement in the penitentiary, not less than two nor more than five years.

Chapter 7 Trading with Slaves

Article 668 shall hereafter read as follows: If any person who deals in intoxicating liquors, either by wholesale or retail, shall sell to a slave without the written consent of his master, mistress, overseer, or employer, any intoxicating liquors, or shall give to any such slave, and without such written consent, any intoxicating liquors, he shall be fined, not less than fifty nor more than two hundred dollars.[131]

Part. III—Title 2

Rules Applicable to Offenses Against the Person When Committed by Slaves or Free Persons of Color

Article 802 shall hereafter read as follows: The offenses enumerated in Title 17 of the second part of the Penal Code, when committed by slaves or free persons of color, against a free white person, are subject to different rules from such as are prescribed in defining such offenses when committed by a free white person, and the guilt or innocence of the accused is to be ascertained by a consideration of following general principles:

1. The right of the master to the obedience and submission of his slave, in all lawful things, is perfect, and the power belongs to the master to inflict any punishment upon the slave not affecting life or limb, and not coming within the definition of cruel treatment or unreasonable abuse, which he may consider necessary for the purpose of keeping him in such submission, and enforcing such submission to his commands; and if, in the

exercise of this right, with or without cause, the slave resists and slays his master, it is murder.
2. The master has not the right to kill his slave, or to maim or dismember him, except in cases mentioned in Article 564 of this Code.
3. A master, in the exercise of his right to perfect obedience on the part of the slave, may correct in moderation, and is the exclusive judge of the necessity for such correction; and resistance by the slave, under such circumstances, if it results in homicide, renders him guilty of murder.
4. The insolence of a slave will justify a white man in inflicting moderate chastisement, with an ordinary instrument of correction, if done at the time when the insolent language is used, or within a reasonable time after; but it will not authorize the excessive battery, as with a dangerous weapon.
5. The rules respecting manslaughter, as given in the second part of this Code, apply only to equals, and not to the case of offenses of slaves, or free persons of color, against free white persons.
6. An assault and battery, not inflicting great injury, committed by a free white person upon a slave, will not be sufficient provocation to mitigate a homicide of the former by the latter, from murder to manslaughter although in a case where the law does not expressly justify such assault and battery.
7. That amount of personal injury is a legal provocation, of which it can be pronounced, having due regard to the relative condition of the white man and slave, and the obligation of the latter to conform his passions to his condition of inferiority, that it would provoke well disposed slaves into a violent passion, and the existence of such provocation will reduce the homicide to manslaughter.

8. If a slave, by insolence, provoke chastisement, and then slay the person chastising him, it will be murder.
9. In the following cases it is lawful for a free person to inflict chastisement upon a slave by moderate whipping:
    (a) If a slave, without the consent of the white person, be found upon his premises at night.
    (b) If the slave, against the orders of the white person, be found upon his premises at any time.
    (c) If a slave be found using improper language, or guilty of indecent or turbulent conduct in the presence of white persons.
    (d) If the slave be guilty of rude or unbecoming conduct in the presence of a free white female.
    (e) If a slave use insulting language or gestures towards a white person.
    (f) If a slave commit any wilful act, Injurious to the property or person of a free white person, or of any member of his family.
    (g) If a slave be found drunk, and making a disturbance in any public place, or upon the premises of a white person.[132]

Laws of Texas. Under the Confederacy, Regulatory of African Slavery
Constitution of the Confederate States of America Article 1, Section 9, Slavery

The importation of negroes of the African race from any foreign country, other than the slave-holding states and territories of the United States of America, is hereby forbidden and Congress is required to pass such laws as shall effectually prevent the same. Congress shall also have power to prevent the introduction of slaves from any state not a member of or territory not belonging to this Confederacy.

No bill of attainder, ex post facto law, or law denying or impairing the right of property in negro slaves shall be passed.[133]

Article IV. Section 2

The citizens of each state shall be entitled to all the privileges and immunities of citizens in the several states, and shall have the right of transit and sojourn in any state of this Confederacy, with their slaves and other property; and the right of property in said slaves not be thereby impaired.

No slave or other person held to service or labor in state or territory of the Confederacy, under the laws thereof, escaping or lawfully carried into another, shall in consequences of any law or regulation therein be discharged from such service or labor, but shall be delivered up on claim of the party to whom such slave belongs, or to whom such service or labor may be due.

Constitution of the State of Texas Confederate States of America
Article 1. Bill of Rights[134]

Section 2: All freemen, when they form social compact, have equal rights; and no man, or set of men, is entitled to separate public emoluments or privileges, but in consideration of public services.

Article III, Legislative Department

Section 1: That all persons who were citizens of the

State of Texas on the second day of March, 1861; all persons bom after that time, of parents citizens of this State; all persons bom in this State of parents residing in and entitled to acquire the rights of citizenship; all citizens of either of the Confederate States of America, or of any State which may hereafter he admitted into union with the Confederate States of America, on terms of equality with them, immigrating to and permanently residing in this State; all persons naturalized by the constitution and laws of the Confederate States of America and of this State, and permanently residing therein, (Indians not taxed, negroes and their descendants excepted), shall be citizens of the State of Texas.

Section 2: All free male citizens of this State, as defined in the preceding section, over the age of twenty-one years, who shall have resided in State one year next preceding an election, and the last six months in the district, county, city, or town in which they offer to vote, shall be deemed qualified electors.

Section 29: The Legislature shall at their first meeting, and in the year 1848 and 1850, and every eight years thereafter, cause an enumeration to be made of all the free inhabitants, (Indians not taxed, Africans and descendants of Africans, excepted), of the State, designating particularly the number of qualified electors; and the whole number of representatives shall, at the several periods of making such enumeration be fixed by the Legislature, and apportioned among the several counties, cities, or towns, according to the number of free population in each; and shall not be less than forty-five nor more than ninety.

Article VIII
Slaves

Section 1: The Legislature shall have no power to pass for the emancipation of slaves.

Section 2: No citizen, or other person residing in this State, shall have power by deed or will, to take effect in State, or out of it, in any manner, whatsoever, directly or indirectly, to emancipate his slave or slaves.

Section 3: The Legislature shall have no power to pass any law to prevent immigrants of this State, from bringing with them such persons of the negro race as are deemed slaves by the laws of any of the Confederate States of America. Provided, that slaves who have committed any felony may be excluded from this State.

Section 4: In the prosecution of slaves for crimes of higher grade that petit larceny, the Legislature shall have no power to deprive them of a trial by jury, except in cases arising under the laws concerning insurrection of slaves.

Section 5: Any person who shall maliciously dismember, or deprive a slave of life, shall suffer such punishment as would be inflicted in case the like offense had been committed upon a free white person, and on the like proof; except when such slave has committed, or attempted to commit rape on a white female, or in case of insurrection of such slave.

Section 6: The Legislature shall have power to pass laws which will oblige the owners of slaves to treat them with humanity.

An Act
Providing for the Disposition of Runaway Slaves

Section 1: That as early as possible after the commitment of a runaway slave, it shall be the duty of the sheriffs of the different counties of the State to cause an advertisement to be published in a newspaper printed nearest the county, or in a newspaper having the largest circulation in the county where the commitment is made, in which shall be a complete description of the slave and any other circumstances calculated to lead to the discovery of the slave by his owner, and if after six months, the owner should not apply for, prove and take out of jail such slave, paying such expenses as are now allowed by law, together with the expense of advertising, the Sheriff shall then convey and deliver such runaway slave to the keeper of the State Penitentiary, and the Sheriff shall at the same time deliver to the financial agent of the Penitentiary a certificate from the Justice of the Peace who committed such runaway slave to jail, stating the amount of charges legally incurred in apprehending and securing such runaway slave, and to whom the same is due.

Section 2: That the Sheriff shall be allowed ten cents per mile in going to and returning from the Penitentiary as a full compensation for conveying such runaway slave thereto, an account of which he shall file with the financial agent.

Section 3: If any sheriff fail to convey any runaway slave to the Penitentiary at the expiration of six months from the time of commitment to jail, such sheriff shall not make any charge for maintaining said runaway slave after said time.

Section 4: It shall be the duty of the keeper of the Penitentiary to receive such runaway slave into custody and advertise as prescribed above for sheriff or until such runaway slave is legally claimed and taken away; if the owner shall fail to come or send for said slave, the slave shall continue in the charge and service of the keeper of the Penitentiary for life: Provided that the owner may at any future time come forward and prove his property, pay the expenses which have accrued up to the time of the delivery of the slave to the keeper of the Penitentiary, and take the slave away.

Section 5: The keeper of the Penitentiary shall certify the delivery of the slave under the provisions of this act to the Controller of Public Accounts, who, upon presentation of such certificate, together with the properly authenticated account of the expenses which may have accrued from the apprehension and confinement of such slave up to the time of the delivery to the keeper of the Penitentiary, shall issue his warrant for the amount, in favor of the Sheriff, which amount shall be paid out of any money in the Treasury of the State, not otherwise appropriated.

Section 6: The keeper of the Penitentiary shall not be allowed to make any charge for receiving, keeping, or feeding any runaway slave committed to his custody, but such slave shall be put to labor as other prisoners.

Section 7: Before any runaway slave shall be delivered up to any person claiming the same, such claimant shall first prove by the affidavit of some disinterested witness that such claimant has lost such a slave as the one described in the advertisement; that the runaway slave is the one he lost; and pay all expenses incurred in apprehending, securing, receiving, maintaining and advertising such runaway. The keeper of the Penitentiary shall deliver any runaway to the owner or his agent, upon his or their complying with the foregoing requisitions, and upon bond and security being given, should be required by the keeper, to indemnify the keeper; and the financial agent shall demand and receive all expenses incurred in the apprehension, recovery, maintaining and advertising such runaway, which amount shall be paid into the State Treasury.

Section 8: The legally authorized agent of any person claiming a runaway slave, may claim, prove and receive such runaway in like manner as the owner is enabled to do by this act.[135]

An Act
To Provide Against the Hostile Invasion of the State of Texas by Persons of Color

Section 1: That any person of color invading or coming into the State of Texas during the present war between the Confederate States and the United States, with any armed force of the enemy, or for purposes of waging war against the people of said State of Texas, or the people of any of the Confederate States, or of exciting insurrection amongst our slaves, or who being within the jurisdiction of said State, shall voluntarily join or be found in the ranks of our enemies, rendering them any character of service, or in any manner whatever giving them aid and comfort, shall be dealt with as is hereinafter provided.

Section 2: Upon the apprehension or capture of any such person by the authorities of the State, it shall be the duty of the State authority, having said person in custody, to notify the Judge of the District Court of his Judicial District of the fact, who shall upon a designated day, not less than ten nor more than twenty days after receiving such notification, examine into the truth of the accusation made; said examination to be had after due notice thereof to the prisoner in the county where said prisoner is detained, and if it shall appear that the prisoner comes under the provisions of the first section of this act, he shall be deemed to have forfeited his freedom, if he is free, and shall be ordered to be confined in the State Penitentiary at labor until the expiration of twelve months after the ratification of a treaty of peace between the Confederate States and the United States, and at the expiration of said period to be dealt with as hereinafter provided.

Section 3: It shall be the duty of the Secretary of State, within sixty days after the ratification of the treaty of peace aforesaid, to procure a complete list of all persons then remaining confined in the Penitentiary under the provisions of this act, with a full description thereof, including the name, age, complexion, height, and weight of such person, and any other peculiar mark by which they may be identified, together with the name and residence, if known, of the alleged owner of such, if any, as claim to be slaves; which said list he shall cause to be published eight successive weeks in newspapers, published in three different portions of the State, one of which shall be at the Capitol of the State, and no two of which shall be published in the same congressional district.

Section 4: At the expiration of twelve months after the ratification of the treaty of peace, a list of all persons remaining in the Penitentiary under the provisions of this act, and not before than reclaimed as runaway slaves, shall be furnished by the Superintendent of the Penitentiary to the Secretary of State, and each person thus remaining shall be remanded to the custody of the Sheriff of the county wherein said Penitentiary is situated, who shall, within sixty days thereafter, expose said person to sale at public auction, before the court house door of said county, to the highest bidder for cash, due notice of the person to be sold and the time, place, and terras of said sale having been first given, by advertisement published eight successive weeks next preceding said sale, in newspapers published, one at the Capital of the State, and one in the county where said sale is to be made, or where no newspaper is published In said county, then in some newspaper published elsewhere in the State, and not at the Capital, having the largest circulation in the county wherein said sale is to be made.

Section 5: The purchase money for each and every person thus sold shall be paid by the purchaser to the Financial Agent of the Penitentiary, and out of the proceeds of said sale the Sheriff shall be entitled to receive the same commissions and fees as are by law allowed in cases of execution, and the balance, if any, after paying all costs, fees, and expenses arising out of the custody, maintenance, advertising and sale of the persons, after leaving the penitentiary, shall be paid into the State Treasury.

Section 6: The Sheriff making a sale of any person under the provisions of this act, shall forewith thereafter make out in duplicate a full and clear account and statement of such sale under his hand, and return one to the Secretary of State and one to the County Clerk of the county wherein such sale was made, who shall record the same among the proper records of evidences of ownership of slaves.

Section 7: The provisions of the laws of the State authorizing free persons of color to choose their masters, or to leave the State, are hereby repealed as to all such persons now in the State, who have invaded the State since the beginning of the present war under the circumstances, or for the purpose specified in Section 1, of this act, and such persons shall be dealt with in all respects according to the provisions of this act: Provided, That it shall not be necessary to have any judicial examination of any such persons as are already confined in the Penitentiary, but such person shall be retained in such confinement for the term prescribed for other cases arising under this act as though they had been originally committed for the period.

Section 8 The owner of any slave held in custody under the provisions of this act may reclaim his property as a runaway slave at any time after said slave has passed into the custody of the State authorities, and before he has been sold: Provided, That the proceedings for the reclamation of such slave shall be had at the cost of the claimant, and before the Chief Justice of the county where said slave may be held in custody at the time said claim is made and be matter of record in said county court, but the right to any person, either slave or free, actually sold as aforesaid, shall be and remain vested in the purchaser of said sale, and the owner of any slave thus sold, shall only, upon proving his property in said slave within three years after said sale, be entitled to receive from the State Treasury the amount paid into said Treasury on account of the sale of said slave.

Section 9: The District Attorney, Sheriff, Clerk, and any other officers whose services may be required in any proceeding arising under the provisions of the second section of this act, or who may have already rendered service in any proceeding in the commitment of any person to the Penitentiary as contemplated in the seventh section of this act, shall be allowed the same fees and expenses as axe allowed in cases of felony.[136]

An Act
To Define the Offense of Inciting Insurrection or Insubordination of Slaves. and to Prescribe the Punishment Therefor

Whereas, in the prosecution of the unholy war now being waged by the United States against the Confederate States and the people thereof, our enemies are seeking to bring upon us a servile war by aiming our slaves and placing them in the ranks of their armies, as well as otherwise, through the action of their government and the commissioned officers of their armies, inciting insurrection and insubordination: Therefore,

Section 1: That it shall be an offense, to be denominated inciting insurrection or insubordination of slaves, for any commissioned officer of the army, navy, or marine service of the government of the United States, during the present war between the United States and the Confederate States, to invade or enter upon, with hostile intent, the territory or soil of this State, or with like intent, to enter within the waters of this State.

Section 2: That any person guilty of inciting insurrection or insubordination, as in this act defined, shall, on conviction thereof, be punished by confinement in the Penitentiary not less than five nor more than fifteen years.

Section 3: This act not being intended to produce any conflict between the State authorities and the government or authorities of the Confederate States, in relation to the management of any matters growing out of the existing war, therefor, only such persons shall be subject to be tried under its provisions as may be, by the proper authorities of the Confederate States, delivered over to the civil authorities of this State, for the purpose of being so tried, and any person convicted under the provisions of this act, shall, at any time after such conviction, on demand made therefor by the President of the Confederate States on the Governor of this State, be delivered up to the proper authorities of the Confederate States.

Section 4: This act is not designated to be in lieu of existing laws defining the exciting or insubordination of slaves, and shall not be construed in any manner to affect such laws.[137]

An Act
To Amend an Act to Amend an Act to Establish a Penal Code.

Approved August 26. 1856; Approved February 12, 1858

Section 1: That Article 34 of "An Act to Amend an Act to Establish a Penal Code," approved August 26, 1856; approved February 12, 1858, be amended so as hereafter to read as follows: All free white persons who have less than one-eighth African blood come within the meaning of the term "Free white persons"; and all free white persons who have that, or a quarter proportion of African blood come within the meaning of the terra, "Free persons of color." Slaves are all such persons of African descent as are held in slavery by the laws of this State, or any of the States or Territories of the Confederate States, or of any foreign country.

Section 2: That Article 349 of said act may be amended as to read as follows: 'Whenever, in the Penal Code or Code of Criminal Procedure, it is declared, that an officer is guilty of an offense, on account of any particular act or omission, and there is not, in the Penal Code, any punishment assigned for the same, should officer shall be deemed guilty of a misdemeanor and shall be fined not exceeding two hundred dollars.

Section 3: That said act be so amended by adding the following article thereto: If any person shall sell, give, or loan, to a slave or slaves, a gun, pistol, bowie knife, or dagger, or any gun-powder or percussion caps, without the written consent of his or her master, mistress, or overseer, he or she shall be confined to hard labor in the Penitentiary not less than two nor more than five years.

Section 4: That Article 745a, of said act, be amended as to read as follows: If any person shall receive or conceal property which has been acquired by another, in such manner as that the acquisition comes within the meaning of the term theft, knowing the same to have been so acquired, he shall be punished in the same manner as, by law, the person stealing the same would be liable to be punished: Provided, That if a free white person shall receive or conceal such property stolen by a slave or free person of color, he shall be punished in the same manner as, by law, a free white person stealing the same would be liable to be punished.

An Act[138]
To Amend an Act Entitled an Act to Amend an Act to Establish a Code of Criminal Procedure for the State of Texas.

Approved August 26 1856: Approved February 15. 1858

Section 1: The Article 644 be amended so as hereafter to read as follows: The following person only is incompetent to testify in criminal actions: A slave or free person of color shall not testify, except where the prosecution is against a person who is a slave or free person of color.

An Act[139]
To Punish Certain Offenses Committed on Sunday

Section 1: That any person who shall compel his or her slaves, children, or apprentices, to labor on the Sabbath, the day known as Sunday, shall be deemed guilty of a misdemeanor, and upon conviction, shall be fined not less than ten nor more than fifty dollars: Provided, That household duties, works of necessity and charity, shall not be prohibited by this act: Provided further, That this act shall not apply to any work done on sugar plantations during the sugar-making season, or any work that may be necessary to save any crop.

An Act[140]
To Prevent Slaves from Exercising Pretended Ownership of Property

Section 1: That it shall be unlawful for any slave owner to knowingly permit any slave to have, or exercise, any pretended ownership of control, in his or her own right, over any horses, cattle, sheep or hogs, within this State. And where any such pretended right of ownership now exists, the master, or other person having the control of such slave, shall, within six months after the passage of this act, dispose of such property by sale or otherwise.

Section 3: The owner offending under the first section of this act, may be indicted and tried in the District Court, and upon conviction, shall be fined in any sum not exceeding the value of the horses, cattle, sheep, goats or hogs, over which such negro may exercise a pretended ownership, or on which such negro shall have a brand or ear mark.[141]

Constitution of the United States
Article XIII

Section 1: Neither slavery nor involuntary servitude, except as a punishment for crime whereof the party shall have been duly convicted, shall exist within the United States, or any place subject to their jurisdiction.

Section 2: Congress shall have power to enforce this article by appropriate legislation.[142]

Bibliography

Books

Barker, Eugene C., *Austin Papers*, 3 Vols., Washington Gov. Printing Office, 1924.

Barker, Eugene C., *History of Texas*, Southwestern Press, Dallas, Texas, 1926.

Biesele, Rudolph Leopold, *The History of the German Settlements in Texas*, Press of Von Bloeck Go., Austin, Texas, 1924.

Bowers, Claude Gernade, *The Tragic Era*, Houghton Mifflin Co., Cambridge, Hass.

Chase, E. B., *The Founders of the Republic*, Merrihew & Gunn, Philadelphia, 1850.

Garrison, George P., *Texas a Contest of Civilization*. Houghton Mifflin Co., New York, 1903.

Goodwin, Cardinal, *Trans-Mississippi West*, D. Appleton cc Co., New York, 1928.

Hart, Albert Bushnell, *Slavery and Abolition*, D. Appleton Co., New York, 1886.

Kennedy, William, *The Rise. Progress. and Prospect of the Republic of Texas*. 2 Vols., R. Hastings Co., London, 1841.

Lowell, James Russell, *Anti-Slavery Papers*, Houghton Mifflin Co., New York, 1908.

Inndy, Benjamine, *The War in Texas*, Merrihew & Gunn, Philadelphia, 1837.

Marquis, James, *The Raven*, The Bobbs-Merrill Co., 1929.

McDonald, William, *Documentary Source Book of American History*, The McMillan Co., New York, 1908.

McLaughlin, Andrew C., Dodd, Arthur, *Source Problems in United States History,* Harper & Bros., New York, 1918.

Olmsted, Frederick Law, *A Journey through Texas*, Dix, Edwards Co., New York, 1882.

Olmsted, Frederick Law, *A Journey in the Seaboard Slave States 1853-1854*, G. P. Putman & Sons, New York, 1887.

Phillips, Ulrich B., *Plantations and Frontier,* Arthur Clark Co., Cleveland, Ohio, 1912.

Phillips, Ulrich B., *American Negro Slavery,* The Crisis Publ. Co., New York, 1918.

Ramsdell, William, *Reconstruction in Texas*, Row, Peterson & Co., Chicago, 1912.

Shippe, Lester Burrell, *Recent American History,* The McMillan Co., New York, 1930.

Smedes, Susan Dabney, *Memoirs of a Plantation,* Houghton Mifflin Co., Cambridge, Mass., 1891.

Smith, Henry, *A Political History of Slavery,* G. P. Putman's Sons, New York, 1903.

Tiling, Moritz, *German Element in Texas,* Moritz Tiling Publ. Co., Houston, Texas, 1913.

Wharton, Clarence R., *History of Texas*, Young Printing Co., Houston, Texas, 1922.

Wooten, Dudley G., *History of Texas*, W. G. Scarff Co*, Chicago, 1898.

Yoakum, H., *History of Texas,* 2 Vols., Redfield Publ. Co., New York, 1856.

Encyclopedias and Law Digests

Gammel, H. P. N., *The Laws of Texas,* A. C. Baldwin & Sons, State Printers, Austin, Texas.

Green, *Complete Digest of Texas Laws,* Brancrof Whitney & Co., San Francisco, Cal.

Michie, Thomas Johnson, *The Encyclopedic Digest of Texas Reports,* Michie Co., Law Publ., Charlottesville, Va., 1911.

Periodicals

Barker, Eugene C., "The African Slave Trade," *Texas State Historical Quarterly VI.*

Bugbee, Lester G.," Slavery in Early Texas," *Political Science Quarterly XIII.*

Curlee, Abigail, "The History of a Texas Slave Plantation," *Southwest Historical Quarterly XXVI.*

Franklin, Lafayette Riley, "The South in the Building of the Nation," *Southern Historical Society XIII.* 1909.

Texas State Documents. Records and Reports

Actas, *Journal of Mexican Legislature,* 1824. The

Archives of Bexar, Reprint from Texas University Record.

Aury, James & R,,, *Letters Concerning; the Slave Trade in Texas,* Texas Archives, Austin, Texas. Assessment Rolls, State Comptroller, Austin, Texas. Census, United States, 1860.

Congress, Laws and Acts, Third, 1839.

Congress, Laws and Acts, Fourth, 1840.

Congress. Laws and Acts, Sixth, 1842.

Congress. Laws and Acts, Eighth, 1844.

Executive Records, *Provisional Government of Texas,* Vol. XXXV.

Legislature. State Laws of Texas, Sessions I-X.

Penal Code of Texas Regarding Slavery, Archives of Texas.

Secession Journal of Texas.

Reconstruction Journal of Texas.

Original Documents

Afleck Papers, 1830-1836, Rosenberg Library, Galveston, Texas.

Blackshear Papers, 1830-1836, Texas Archives, Austin, Texas.

Bolton, J. T., *Diary & Plantation Records*, Texas Archives, Austin, Texas.

Brown, Henry, *Letter to Sister, 1843.* Texas Archives, Austin, Texas.

Chambers Papers, 1805-1900. Texas Archives, Austin, Texas.

Fisher Papers, 1830-1839. Texas Archives, Austin, Texas.

Kleberg Papers, 1838-1873. Texas Archives, Austin, Texas.

Menefee Letters, 184Q-1843. Texas Archives, Austin, Texas.

Nicholson Papers, 1838-1850. Texas Archives, Austin, Texas.

Perry Papers, Texas Archives, Austin, Texas.

Piper Papers, Texas Archives, Austin, Texas.

Seward Papers, Texas Archives, Austin, Texas.

Tait Papers, Texas Archives, Austin, Texas.

Thornhill Papers, Texas Archives, Austin, Texas.

Newspapers

Democratic Telegraph & Texas Register, 1846-1853.

Galveston Weekly News, July 24, 1855; April 3, 1860.

Houston Price Current & Business Register, Jan. 8, 1857.

Houston Republic, 1857, 1858.

Houston Telegraph, Aug. 18, 1860.

Houston Chronicle, Sept. 11, 1926.

Southern Intelligencer, Austin, Texas, Dec. 12, 1860.

The Morning Star, Apr. 8, 1839; Oct. 26, 1844.

Telegraph & Texas Register, Oct. 10, 1835; April 14, 1836; August 11, 1838; March 4, 1846.

Texas Monument of LaGrange, Texas, July 28, 1852; June 21, 1854; August 1, 1854.

Texas Gazette. 1829-1831.

Texas Republican. July, 1834.

True Issue, LaGrange, Texas, Dec. 22, 1860; Feb. 4, 1861; March 14, 1861.

Washington American, Washington, Texas, Nov. 1, 1855; Oct. 29, 1856.

Manuscripts

Reed, J. M., *"Reminiscences,"* Texas Archives.

Union Nat'l. Bank, *Early History of Harris County,* 1928.

Masterson, J. H., *Texas Plantations.*

MS No. 149, Texas State Library, Austin, Texas.

Miscellaneous

Texas Almanac, 1858.

Reminiscences of Sarah, Slave in Brazoria County.

Personal Observation in Brazoria and Wharton Counties.

Personal Interviews.

1. I am grateful to Flora von Roeder's book, *These are the Generations*, Volume II, ISBN 978-1497599345 together with help from Charlotte Hill of New Braunfels and information relayed by Martha Rutherford about her great aunt.
2. Sigismund Engelking had been one of the first two pupils and later taught in the school in Millheim run by E.G. Maetze. From: Woodrick and Engelking (2017), *The Millheim and Cat Spring Pioneers— German Immigrants Building a New Life in Texas* p.75. ISBN: 978-1-9998691-2-0. He also enlisted as a Confederate (CSV) private in the 1st Texas Infantry in Company F at the age of 18 being severely wounded in the action at Sharpsburg on 1 September 1862. (https://antietam.aotw.org/officers.php?officer_id=1472)
3. *The Cat Spring Story* (1959), Cat Spring Agricultural Society, p. 34.
4. In Memoriam Helen (Engelking) Handley, *The Austin Chronicle*, Fri., Nov. 15, 2002. Listen also to: https://marfapublicradio.org/blog/rambling-boy/sigismund-engelking-ranch-stories/
5. Also of note is that the Rice Hotel was completed in 1913 on the site of the former Capitol building of the Republic of Texas. As the daughter of the Republic of Texas this would be most relevant! According to a Wikipedia article: "It continued to operate as a hotel before finally shutting down in 1977. After standing vacant for twenty-one years, The Rice was renovated as apartments and reopened in 1998 as the Post Rice Lofts. It was sold in 2014 and renamed simply The Rice".
6. https://emuseum.jfk.org/objects/33018
7. Barker, Eugene C., History of Texas, p. 132
8. Barker, Eugene C., Op. cit,. p. 145
9. Bancroft, *History of Mexico*, p. 79
10. *Bexar Archives*. MS No. 14., University of Texas
11. Census. Jan. 26, 1818, MS *Bexar Archives*, University of Texas
12. Barker, *Life of Austin*, p. 146
13. *Archives*. University of Texas
14. *Archives of Texas*. University of Texas
15. Gammel, *The Laws of Texas*. Vol. I, pp. 78-79
16. Gammel, H. P. op. Cit., Vol. I, pp. 78-79
17. *Austin Papers,* Part II, p. 1405
18. *Ibid.*
19. *Ibid.*, p. 1066
20. Gammel, op. Cit., Vol. I, p. 323
21. *Texas Report,* Vol. II, p. 342
22. *Austin Papers,* Original Manuscript, Texas University Library, Austin, Texas

23 *Georgia Courier,* Augusta, Ga., July 3, 1828
24 Phillips, U. B., *Plantation and Frontier,* p. 96
25 Bugbee, *Slavery in Early Texas,* p. 98
26 Kennedy's Texas, Almonte's *Statistical Notice.* pp. 11, 75-76
27 Kennedy's *Texas,* Almonte's *Statistical Report,* pp. 11, 75-76
28 Bugbee, *Slavery in Texas*, Political Science Quarterly mi. pp. 662-663
29 *Ibid.*, pp. 81-86
30 *Austin Papers,* Part I, p. 686
31 *Ibid.*, p. 792
32 *The Austin Papers,* Part I, p. 701
33 *Ibid.*, p. 803
34 *The Austin Papers*, Part I, p. 982
35 *Ibid.*, p. 919
36 *Ibid.*, p. 919
37 Lundy, Benjamine, *The War in Texas.* p. 83
38 *Virginia Journal Session,* 1832
39 *Ibid.*, 1832
40 Gammel, *Laws of Texas,* p. 28
41 *Austin Papers*, Vol. III, p. 190
42 Gammel, Op. Cit., p. 34
43 Wharton, Clarence, History of Texas, p. 283
44 Wooten, *History of Texas*, Vol. I, p. 1685-1745
45 Kennedy, Wm., *Texas,* Vol. I, p. 168
46 *Southwestern Historical Quarterly,* Vol. XXVIII, p. 221
47 *Austin Papers*. Part II, p. 1086
48 *Ashbel Smith Papers,* Archives University of Texas
49 *Ibid.*
50 *Ibid.*
51 *Austin Papers,* Part II, p. 462
52 *Private Collection*, Old Land Office, Austin, Texas
53 Gammel, *Texas Laws* Vol. VI, p. 183
54 *Journals of the Fourth Congress of the Republic of Texas,* 1839-1840, Archives Texas State Library
55 Memorial No. 101. File Box 67, Archives State Dept.
56 Hawren, Alleine, *Causes and Origin of the Decree of Apr. 6. 1830. Forbidding American Emigrants,* Southwestern Historical Quarterly, 1912-1913, XII, p. 383-387
57 *29th Congress, 2cd Session, Congressional Globe,* p. 495
58 *National Intelligencer,* Oct. 31, 1844
59 *Ibid.*
60 Garrison, *Diplomatic Correspondence of Republic of Texas,* Vol. I, p. 127-135.
61 *25th Congress, 1st Session, House Document,* No. 40 p. 11-13

62 Smith, Justin H., *The Annexation of Texas*, p. 79
63 Smith, Justin H., Op. Cit., p. 84
64 *Ibid.*, p. 94
65 *Ibid.*, p. 97
66 *Ibid.*, p. 110
67 Smith, J. H., Op. Cit., p. 465
68 Masterson, J. H., *Texas Plantations,* MS, Union National Bank, Houston, Texas
69 Perry, Mrs. J. H., and Sarah, who is a slavery-time negro, Brazoria County, Texas, *A Personal Visit and Interview* on the old plantation.
70 Personal Observations and *Houston Chronicle* of September 11, 1926
71 Texas Archives, *Tait Papers,* Texas University, Austin, Texas
72 *Tait Papers*, Texas Library, University of Texas, Austin, Texas, Original Documents
73 *Austin Papers,* Texas Library, Univ. of Texas, Austin, Texas, Original Documents
74 *Telegraph and Texas Register.* Oct. 2, 1848
75 Sarah, Slavery-time negro, Brazoria County, Texas Personal Interview
76 *Piper Papers*, Original Document, Univ. of Texas, Austin, Texas
77 *Piper Papers*, Original Document, Univ. of Texas, Austin, Texas
78 *State Comptroller's Roll*, State Capitol, Austin, Texas
79 *Eighth Census of United States,* 1860
80 *State Comptroller's Office,* Assessment Rolls, Austin, Texas
81 *Texas Almanac, 1858,* County Statistics
82 *Assessment Rolls of State Comptroller's*, Austin, Texas
83 *Piper Papers*, Texas University Library, Austin, Texas
84 *Texas Reports,* Vol. 4, p. 266
85 *Texas Reports,* Vol. 4, p. 444
86 *Texas Reports,* Vol. 6, p. 369
87 *Ibid.*, p. 383
88 *The Houston Telegraph*, Aug. 18, 1860
89 *Journal of Secession,* 1861
90 Journal *of Secession,* 1861
91 *Secession Journal of Texas.* 1861, p. 61-62
92 *Encyclopedic Digest of Texas Reports,* Vol. 15, p. 759
93 Reed, A. P., *Reminiscences of Bell County,* MS No. 492 Archives of Texas, Texas University Library, Austin
94 Masterson, J. H., Personal Interview, Houston, Texas
95 *Archives of Texas,* MS No. 129, Library of University of Texas, Austin, Texas
96 *Texas Reports,* Vol. 31, p. 504-523
97 McDonald, *Documentary Source Book of American History,* p. 439
98 *Texas State Library* MS 149, State Capitol, Austin, Texas

99 *Executive Records, Provisional Government,* Vol. 35, p. 66-67
100 *Executive Records, Provisional Government*
101 *Executive Records. Provisional Government*, Vol. 35, p. 5-7
102 Laws of the Republic, Vol. 1, p. 187
103 Laws of the Republic, Vol. 1, p. 232
104 Laws of the Republic, Vol. 1, p. 239
105 *Ibid.*, p. 234
106 *The Law of the Republic*, Vol. 2, p. 43
107 *The Laws of the Republic,* Vol. 3, p. 12
108 First Session of Third Congress MS 1839, p. 46
109 Laws of the Fourth Congress, MS 1840, p. 151
110 *Laws of the Republic,* 1841, p. 4
111 *Laws of the Republic,* 1841, p. 51
112 *Laws of the Republic,* Sixth Congress, 1842, p. 25
113 *Laws of the Republic,* Eighth Congress, MS, 1844, p. 38-39
114 *Laws of Texas*, Volume II, p. 5
115 *Laws of the Second Legislature,* p. 29
116 *Ibid.*, p. 99-102
117 *Laws of the Second Legislature,* p. 133
118 *Laws of the Third Legislature,* p. 4
119 *Laws of the Fourth Legislature,* p. 20
120 *Laws of the Fourth Legislature,* p. 33
121 *Laws of the Fifth Legislature,* p. 10
122 *Laws of the Fifth Legislature*, p. 59
123 *Ibid.*, p. 67
124 *Laws of the Sixth Legislature*, p. 83-84
125 *Laws of the Sixth Legislature,* Adjourned Session, p. 81
126 *Laws of the Seventh Legislature,* p. 75
127 *Laws of the Seventh Legislature*, p. 202
128 *Acts of the Legislature,* August 28, 1856
129 *Penal Code of Texas,* p. 110-111
130 *Penal Code of Texas,* p. 114-120
131 *Laws of the Seventh Legislature,* p. 156-189
132 *Laws of the Seventh Legislature,* p. 213-216
133 *The South in the Building of the Nation,* Vol. IV, p. 258
134 *Gamel's Laws of Texas,* Vol. V, p. 3
135 *Laws of the Eighth Legislature,* Special Session, p. 49
136 *Laws of the Eighth Legislature,* Special Session, p. 20
137 *Laws of the Eighth Legislature,* Special Session, p. 33
138 *Laws of the Ninth Legislature,* Extra Session, p. 18
139 *Laws of the Ninth Legislature,* First Called Session, p. 12
140 *The Laws of the Ninth Legislature.* First Called Session, p. 24
141 *The Laws of the Tenth Session,* First Called Session, p. 16

www.ingramcontent.com/pod-product-compliance
Lightning Source LLC
LaVergne TN
LVHW032010070526
838202LV00059B/6385

9783949197963